Living in the New Consciousness

Living in the New Consciousness

Hugo Enomiya-Lassalle

Edited by Roland Ropers

Translated from the German by
Paul Shepherd

Foreword by David Steindl-Rast, O.S.B.

Shambhala
Boston & Shaftesbury
1988

SHAMBHALA PUBLICATIONS, INC.
Horticultural Hall
300 Massachusetts Avenue
Boston, Massachusetts 02115

SHAMBHALA PUBLICATIONS, INC.
The Old School House
The Courtyard, Bell Street
Shaftesbury, Dorset SP7 8BP

© 1986 by Kösel-Verlag GmbH & Co., Munich
Translation © 1988 by Shambhala Publications, Inc.
Foreword © 1988 by David Steindl-Rast, O.S.B.

9 8 7 6 5 4 3 2 1

First Edition

Printed in the United States of America

Distributed in the United States by Random House
and in Canada by Random House of Canada Ltd.
Distributed in the United Kingdom by Element Books Ltd.

LIBRARY OF CONGRESS
Library of Congress Cataloging-in-Publication Data

Enomiya-Lassalle, Hugo M. (Hugo Makibi), 1898–
    [Leben im neuen Bewusstsein. English]
    Living in the new consciousness / Hugo Enomiya-Lassalle;
translated from the German by Paul Shepherd.—1st ed.
    p. cm.
    Translation of: Leben im neuen Bewusstsein.
    ISBN 0-87773-449-6 (pbk.)
    1. Spiritual life. 2. Consciousness—Religious aspects. 3. Zen
Buddhism. I. Title.
BL624.E5613 1988
291.4—dc19   88-15797
                                                      CIP

CONTENTS

FOREWORD   ix

ACKNOWLEDGMENTS   xiii

INTRODUCTION   xv

PART ONE.   *Humanity at the Turning Point*   1

1. Where Is Humanity Going?   3
2. The Way from Archaic to Rational Consciousness   5
3. The New Integral Consciousness   8
4. Time-Freedom, Transparency, and Holistic Experience   9
5. Transparency, or The Current Exigency as a Symptom of
   Crisis   11
6. What Can and Should Be Done?   12
7. The Hour of Birth for the New Man   15
8. A New Way of Thinking and a New Uprightness   17
9. The Forerunners, Tauler and Eckhart: Returning to
   Mysticism   19

PART TWO.   *The Dimensions of Cosmic Consciousness*   21

10. Mystical Experience and Scientific Discovery   25
11. The Present Crisis as a Harbinger of the Fourth
    Dimension of Consciousness   28
12. Becoming a Part of the Whole through Freedom from
    Ego   30
13. Prevailing over Space and Time: How to Cope with Stress
    and Cancer   31
14. Prophetic Elements in the Arts   34
15. The Fourth Dimension   36
16. The Theory of Relativity, or Prevailing over Materialism   39
17. Transcending Dualism in the Field of Biology   43

18. Open Thinking, or The End of Philosophy 45
19. The New Consciousness and Unconscious Archetypes, or
    Avoiding Atomic War 47
20. Teilhard de Chardin: Eastern Roads, Western Roads 49

PART THREE. *Transformation of Religious Consciousness* 53
21. The Transformation of Consciousness 55
22. Transformations in Consciousness in Karl Jaspers' "Axial
    Period" 58
23. The Present Threat: Nonsimultaneity in the
    Transformation 62
24. Finding the Way Back to Our Religious Roots 65
25. New Access to the Scriptures 67
26. The Spiritual Vacuum in the West and What the East Has
    to Offer 69
27. Sri Aurobindo: Concrete Steps in Education Toward
    Transformation of Religious Consciousness 72

PART FOUR. *Meditation and the Experience of God* 77
28. An Answer to the Longing for Meditation 81
29. Initial Difficulties 84
30. Beginning the Practice of Meditation 87
31. From Objective to Nonobjective Meditation 92
32. Cistern Water and Spring Water: Two Ways to Experience
    God 95
33. Mystical Experience, East and West 97
34. The Third Eye of the Mystic and the Experience of Hugh
    of Saint-Victor 99

PART FIVE. *Zen and Christianity* 101
35. What Is Zen? 103
36. The Origin of Zazen 104
37. The Practice of Zen Meditation 106
38. The Master 113
39. Goals and Effects 115
40. Enlightenment 121
41. Kosen Imakita: "Like One Risen from the Dead" 124

PART SIX. *The Transparency of God in Everyday Life* 127
42. The Divine Milieu 129
43. Hope in the Present Crisis: Transparency of the Divine in the New Man 131
44. The New Consciousness in Everyday Life 134
45. "Yes to Christ but No to the Church": The Search for the Dwelling Place of Divine Reality 137
46. The Cloud of Unknowing: Coming to Our Spiritual Home in Everyday Life 143

HUGO M. ENOMIYA-LASSALLE: A BIOGRAPHICAL SKETCH 149

A NOTE ON ZEN SESSHIN 153

Foreword

To my embarrassment I cannot even remember when and where I met Father Enomiya-Lassalle for the first time. My memory for biographical details leaves much to be desired. But there are moments when everyday experience fuses with an archetypal image. Those moments last. We cannot forget them. My heart holds an image of that kind from one of my early encounters with Father Enomiya-Lassalle. He, the great teacher, had invited the young monk I was for a walk. We had climbed the highest hill far and wide. Below us the monastery deep down there: its steeple, its farm, the cows, the tractor, all in miniature, like a child's toy. The town and the highway still farther away, lost in the mist along the river. Around us, up here, sunlight and the silence of high places. Our conversation—though I cannot recall one word of it—high.

Recently, we shared a platform at a congress in Europe. Decades had passed. Father Enomiya-Lassalle's book *Zen: Way to Enlightenment* had gone through half a dozen editions. Its author was close to ninety by now. But, as soon as he started speaking, my heart stood again on that high hill. Martin Luther King, Jr., flashed into my mind; he had "been to the mountain." Moses, who entered the Cloud of God's Presence high on Mount Sinai. Jesus, who went up to a high mountain to pray and started to shine. Precisely because he is so totally unassuming, Father Enomiya-Lassalle strikes one as a man at home on the heights.

Seen from a mountain peak, the landscape reveals its basic features. Nonessentials lose importance; essentials stand out. Father Enomiya-Lassalle's insights, gathered in this book, show the clarity of mountain vision, a sense of what matters. What matters most to the youthful mind of this survivor of Hiroshima is a new consciousness. It matters most to him because it is for all of us, aware or unaware, a matter of life or death. Father Enomiya-Lassalle's awareness is the awareness of a man who glimpsed in that flash "brighter than a thousand suns" the very edge of history. Yet others survived that blinding explosion and still lack awareness. His awareness comes out of an *im*plosion, out of the Zen Experience.

The high point that gives this man of vision his perspective is common ground shared by Buddhists and Christians. He is a pioneer of Buddhist-Christian dialogue. The dynamics of that dialogue force us to face the question of common ground. In a first round of exchanges the basic question is, "What do you really mean?" In a second round, however, we cannot avoid asking, "And how do you know?" How *do* we know? Can we agree on a touchstone to test our convictions? What could it be? Father Enomiya-Lassalle knows the answer: The touchstone is experience.

The strength, the depth, the universality of his insights, all three spring from one and the same source: his own mystic experience. A basic definition of mysticism will do for our purposes here. We are speaking of "an experiential awareness of communion with Ultimate Reality." (Read this again. Every word of our definition counts.)

Christians conceive Ultimate Reality in theistic, Buddhists in nontheistic terms; for Zen, this distinction does not matter. What does matter is the experience of ultimate Belonging. Christians speak of Conversion, Buddhists of Enlightenment. Either experience may come suddenly or step by step. Again, this does not matter. What matters is that an experience stands at the heart of Buddhism as well as Christianity. And this experience is, in the strictest sense, mystical.

The life force of saints and of Zen masters alike flowed from the wellspring of mystic experience. But that same spring wells up in every human heart. It may be walled in or reduced to a trickle; it may be muddied or frozen; but it never runs dry. In each one of us it surges up in spurts, once in a while. Even psychology has studied these peak experiences. But this life force need not be left to an "unattended moment" here and there. It can be freed, purified; its flow can be maintained. That is what spiritual practice is all about.

Both Buddhists and Christians find Zen a most helpful method for inner spring cleaning. In the process of this heart labor, they make an astounding discovery: Those whose life is nourished by that wellspring become better Christians by Christian standards and better Buddhists by Buddhist ones. (At that point, they take those labels lightly.) They realize that the Buddhist as well as the Christian path has one goal: "the human being, fully alive." They realize also this: In the measure in which we come alive, we become alive and alert also to the needs of others. Becoming fully human is a task we share with all; it cannot be accomplished in isolation.

It is in this light that Father Enomiya-Lassalle understands Jesus Christ and his Church as the breakthrough of a new consciousness. That is why he can help those who are attracted by Jesus yet put off by the Church; those who understand Jesus yet do not understand the Church. He understands both of them, is committed to both of them. Jesus Christ took him up unto the mountain of his Transfiguration. It is from up there that he looks at Church structures—a steeple, cows, a tractor—"of little importance, though never indifferent." After all, in the light of the Transfiguration on Mount Tabor, even Peter wanted to build no more than three bough sheds, wayfarers' shelters. A Catholic Christian, a Jesuit priest in good standing (or should I say "in good going"?), Father Enomiya-Lassalle knows Jesus Christ as the Way. And he knows that no one is "on the way," no one stays on the way, except by leaving the way behind with every step.

The path for which this book provides signposts (no more, but no less) is the path of a new consciousness. The author has followed that path for a long time. What he sees from the peak he has reached in a vision of peace. Like Moses looking from afar at the Land of Promise with a bittersweet joy, Father Enomiya-Lassalle sees and points out a place which another generation must make its home. There is a task worthy of our enthusiasm.

The author's own enthusiasm is contagious.

Brother David Steindl-Rast, O.S.B.
Hinterthal, Austria
April 28, 1988

Acknowledgments

Grateful acknowledgment is made to the author and the publishers listed below for permission to gather excerpts from the following writings and talks by Hugo Makibi Enomiya-Lassalle.

"Aperspektivistische Wirklichkeitserfahrung und Manifestationen des Aperspektivistischen." Address delivered before the Evangelical Academy, Locum, West Germany, 5 June 1985. Chapters 2, 3, 4, 5, 10, 13, 14, 16, 17, 18, 19.

Meditation als Weg zur Gotteserfahrung. Mainz: Matthias-Grünewald Verlag, 1980. Chapters 28, 29, 30, 32, 33, 46.

"Verändert die Praxis des Zen das religiöse Bewusstsein?" In *Stille Fluchten: Zur Veränderung des religiösen Bewusstseins.* Ed. Knut Walf. Munich: Kösel Verlag, 1983. Chapters 21, 22, 23, 24, 25, 26, 34, 41.

Wohin geht der Mensch? Zurich, Einsiedeln, Cologne: Benziger Verlag, 1981. Chapters 1, 6, 7, 8, 9, 11, 12, 15, 20, 27, 42, 43, 44, 45.

Zen-Meditation: Eine Einführung. Zurich, Einsiedeln, Cologne: Benziger Verlag, 1977. Chapter 32.

Chapters 35–40 (on the practice of Zen meditation) were taken from various talks given by Enomiya-Lassalle in 1985 and 1986.

INTRODUCTION

These readings have been selected from the books, unpublished writings, and speeches of Hugo Makibi Enomiya-Lassalle, a German priest who is also well known as a Zen master. Like his renowned fellow Jesuit the late Teilhard de Chardin, Enomiya-Lassalle is one of the heralds of a new consciousness that will bring us to an experience of absolute reality leading us toward the Omega point of unity with God.

Ever since he began Zen meditation in 1943, Enomiya-Lassalle has been forging the way to God's essence by transcending the exclusively rational and discursive thinking still so dominant today. Over the years, through the force of his personal magnetism as well as that of his writings, he has led people from all over the world along this same path to a new experience of reality. Now eighty-nine years old, Father Enomiya-Lassalle continues to travel tirelessly between Japan and Europe, between East and West, as Zen master and meditation teacher, as religious philosopher and a new type of missionary, trailblazing the path to the new consciousness.

As the result of his continuing dialogue with Buddhists, Father Lassalle has opened a window to the East for many Christians. The Japanese name that he took in 1948, Makibi Enomiya, confirms the intensity of this dialogue. In spite of considerable opposition within his own church, Father Lassalle has rediscovered the wisdom of the East for Christianity while at the same time finding a new avenue to Christian mysticism through his practice of Zen meditation.

Together with his other accomplishments, Enomiya-Lassalle's encounter with Zen has undoubtedly played a consid-

erable part in restoring Christian mystics of the past, such as
Meister Eckhart, Johannes Tauler, Theresa of Ávila and Saint
John of the Cross, to their rightful place in Christian con-
sciousness so they may be understood in all their profundity.

Nothing else in the Church today can compare with the
effect that Father Lassalle's activities have had in reconciling
the religious consciousnesses of East and West. Carl Friedrich
von Weizsäcker, the noted German physicist and philosopher,
wrote of Enomiya-Lassalle's personality: "The encounter
among the world's cultures and particularly the religious
understandings bequeathed by those cultures appears to me
to be one of the most important spiritual developments of our
time. The fact that a man can be, simultaneously and most
authentically both a practicing Jesuit priest and a recognized
Zen master seems to me to be a model of what can happen in
this sphere."

Those who have met this totally unassuming Jesuit priest or
have read his writings have sensed the spiritual dimension of a
man with true mystical experience. In the *Tao Te Ching* of
Lao-tzu we find words that perfectly describe Enomiya-Lassalle himself. "Quietness is called submission to Fate; What
has submitted to Fate has become part of the always-so. To
know the always-so is to be Illumined."*

The unlimited tolerance and profound wisdom of Master
Enomiya-Lassalle can be seen in his association and ongoing
dialogue with his meditation students and the readers of his
books. Rather than seeking out students or partners in dialogue who are in accord with his own religious convictions, he
respects from the start the differing religious roots of each
individual. In Zen meditation under his guidance, each person
finds the way back to his or her own authentic religiosity: in
this way one is "bound" (Latin; *religio*) to one's own true self.
Enomiya-Lassalle constantly reminds his students that the
encounter with God, the experience of the absolute, is a

*Waley, Arthur, *The Way and Its Power: A Study of the Tao Te Ching and
Its Place in Chinese Thought* (London, 1934), p. 162.

principle at work in ourselves. "The Kingdom of God is within you" (Luke 17:21).

It is often difficult to integrate these simple words and make them our own; intellect and rationality so decisively rule our world, leaving little room for the intuitive. Thus Enomiya-Lassalle has something of special worth to offer people today: direction and guidance along the path of Zen meditation toward an experience of one's true self. Like the great mystics of the past, Enomiya-Lassalle also seeks tirelessly the ways and means to become more truly human and distinguishes clearly between the true and the false in spiritual life. While building a bridge between East and West, he has gradually discovered a new spirituality, one that can provide us with the stability we need as we seek our bearings in a confusing world.

Through my many encounters with Father Enomiya-Lassalle, both in Zen meditation courses and in personal conversation, I have experienced the great power of his guidance along the spiritual path. Every sentence, every bit of advice, every gesture comes from a man whose whole life embodies truth and the genuine imitation of Christ. The celebrations of the Eucharist that I have attended under Enomiya-Lassalle remain unforgettable experiences for me, as for most of the participants. The stark simplicity of the ceremony and the depth of his words are eloquent testimony to a true master, a host who gathers his friends at the Lord's table and initiates a union with God that can be felt.

The apostles of Christ and the countless mystics who followed him, both men and women, experienced the opening of the heart to the inner light, as a release from ignorance and the bondage of suffering. Like Paul, they could say, "Christ lives in me" (Gal. 2:20) or experience through Jesus that "I and the Father are one" (John 10:30). Because we rely more on our heads than our hearts, the goal of this path lies far away. Enomiya-Lassalle leads the seeker in meditation back to the original source, where the mirror of the soul once again becomes clear and transparent. This awakening to the brightness of the inner light is a necessary step in the full spiritual development of the person, of *every* person, a step in which the transcendental sense awakens, the inner eye opens, and reality is finally encountered. It is a breaking forth from the constricting shell of ego-consciousness, an opening to the breadth and fullness of life found in cosmic consciousness.

In his encounter with the Eastern practice of Zen meditation, Enomiya-Lassalle has rediscovered for Western man the significance of sitting in absolute silence. The Christian mystics already knew about this experience, so valuable for one's inner life. Meister Eckhart writes:

> The person who sits is more ready to bring forth clear things than someone who walks or stands. Sitting means peace. Thus we should sit, which is bowing in humility among all creatures. Then the individual comes to a quiet peace. He reaches this peace in light. The light is given to him in the silence wherein he sits and dwells.

In Johannes Tauler we find a similar passage:

> It is helpful that the outer person be in a state of rest, that he sit and be silent and also be free of unrest in his external body. As a result of this stillness, God will give you the Kingdom of Heaven and Himself.

Like his predecessors who were often misunderstood in their own times, Enomiya-Lassalle is a mystic of our time. His way to cosmic consciousness has as its goal a totally new life. From the sleeper will emerge the awakened one, from the child a spiritual adult, from the seeker of light the enlightened one—the brother of Christ. To walk together with Enomiya-Lassalle along this way is a welcome challenge for people of today. Finding the way back to our origin means finding the way back from distress and disorientation to a true sense of being "at home." In these selected texts, some of which appear for the first time, Enomiya-Lassalle does not lead us to an isolated and elitist "otherworldliness." Nor does he point the way to a withdrawn monkish existence. He is far more concerned with experiencing the present: *"Age quod agis"* ("What you do, do that"). This means being totally present and aware in every moment of being and doing rather than being lost in thoughts of the past or the future. The Zen meditation outlined in this book leads to reality and the present moment. In no way is it a narcissistic preoccupation with finding oneself; on the contrary, it is a way to overcome the obstructing ego. The texts selected here provide hints on how we can find our way to the human center in our active everyday lives and integrate our religious position into the cosmic consciousness of today.

The encounter with Enomiya-Lassalle leads to a remarkable reassessment of such mundane things as discipline, will, concentration, dealing with pain, wordless comprehension, and action without express reward. The method of Zen meditation is to practice with our very human existence, a practice for every day of our lives.

In his talks Enomiya-Lassalle emphasizes that "marriage is more important than Zen." Zen is not an alternative to everyday life; its value is as a completing adjunct to it. With increasing experience in Zen, our attention will improve as will our relations with our brothers and sisters and, indeed, with our whole environment. A new existence, a deeper life in a new consciousness, will make itself felt without any visible or unusual outer signs.

May the following selections testify to the significance that this new consciousness has for us today; may they help to make it possible for many more to share in the great wisdom and tireless creative energy of the apostle and Zen master Enomiya-Lassalle.

Roland Ropers
Düsseldorf
March 1986

PART ONE

HUMANITY AT THE TURNING POINT

Humanity today finds itself in a crisis at the now crossroads between the old consciousness and the new. Today, standing at the threshold of a great evolutionary shift, we encounter the dawn of a better world. A profound transformation is occurring in our thought, our value systems and in our perception of ourselves and our environment. Indeed, we speak nowadays of a "paradigm shift." In the course of centuries of development, man has moved through various stages of consciousness, progressing from an archaic consciousness to a rational consciousness to a new integral consciousness, which last stage includes the fourth dimension. A totally new experience of reality, free from the bounds of space and time, is about to reveal itself. But we will need to overcome conceptual time if we are to press on to an all-embracing perception of the essence of things.

The present crisis is a sign that warns us of the need for transformation and a new orientation. We must gradually free ourselves from our fixation on the three-dimensional, must escape the clock time that imprisons us to become free from time. This will lead to a new stage in human development; the new man's hour of birth, for which the period of labor has already begun. The new thinking will be characterized by uprightness and freedom from preju-

dice, since only in this way will true love among people be possible.

In this process, the teachings of the great mystics, such as Meister Eckhart, Johannes Tauler, Teresa of Ávila and Saint John of the Cross, take on new significance. For the thinking of the new man will be mystical thinking.

> In the eternal birth that occurs in the core and innermost regions of the soul, God covers the soul with light, whereby the light grows so great in the core of our being that it overflows into the faculties of the soul and into the outer person.
>
> [Meister Eckhart]

1

Where Is Humanity Going?

Where is humanity going? This is *the* question of our time, though it may be expressed in the most varied ways. In most cases the question is tinged with concern, not only about individual groups but also about mankind as a whole. Many indeed are the problems and issues that affect not only individuals but also groups of people often numbering in the millions. We need but consider the hunger and uprootedness that we learn of every day through the newspaper, radio, and television. Naturally much is undertaken to alleviate need. But even when this is hardly sufficient, there is nevertheless hope that the situation will inprove in particular areas of the globe. However, in most cases any solution is dependent on relations between nations and all too frequently a crisis has its roots in political tensions. Sometimes the root causes are found in natural catastrophes such as earthquakes and floods, the effects of which can only be partially prevented through human endeavors.

Our question concerns all of humanity and not just individual groups of people. This is certainly no secret today to the careful observer. Humanity stands at a turning point. We could even say that we find ourselves in the midst of a transformation of such dimensions that it occurs only once in millennia. We need but reflect on the difference in the thinking of today's youth and that of their elders, a gap that surely has never been experienced to such a great degree. Logical argumentation is still convincing for most people of the older generation, but it often makes little if any impression on youth. It holds no interest for them. And this is not due to a lack of ability or desire to understand on their part. What is happening? How can this be explained? Reasons for the present transformation lie deeper than we think. It can be said without exaggeration that a seemingly insurmountable wall exists between young and old.

We do not wish here to inquire into the moral defects of mankind and make suggestions about how to cure them. We are much more concerned with determining how the situation stands at present for man, regardless of whether he is responsible for this situation or not. Only then can we begin to ask about what can be done and what outlook there is for our future.

Also typical of the present situation is the widespread discussion about a possible final cataclysm spelling world destruction. Many comfort themselves in the hope that we shall be able somehow to carry on after having emigrated to some far-flung star, where this time we shall not make the same mistakes. This accounts perhaps for the interest in the various religious prophecies about the end of the world. Christ himself spoke of a Last Judgment at the end of time, a subject treated in greater detail in the Revelations of Saint John. We consciously separate ourselves from any interpretation of such eschatologies. We are concerned not with a final step but rather with a new consciousness that appears to be developing. . . .

What is needed now is not a new system. The point is how to overcome the crisis that we face today. There is no system to do this. Many people, still not clear on this fact, evidently think that humanity will be saved from the ruin that threatens it through one of the existing systems, be it communism, capitalism, democracy, or some yet-to-be-discovered form. But in humanity's present crisis we are not concerned with a particular mode of thinking or ideology. Thus it is not our intention to express our opinions about the various ideologies or systems in connection with this.

2

The Way from Archaic to Rational Consciousness*

We shall examine first of all the stages of consciousness. Although this obviously can be only a brief outline, it is still worthy of our attention.

The term *archaic consciousness* refers to the first stage of human consciousness. It is the stage of consciousness constituting the crossover from animal to human, although it is still not possible at this stage to make a sharp distinction between the two. Le Comte de Nouy believes that the crossover point was the moment in which the animal (or the being that eventually emerged as man) became aware of a certain inner freedom that it had not possessed up to then. Up to that point it had been guided solely by instinct or, more precisely, by what we now call instinct. Although we cannot imagine what this was like, for this being it signified a totally new world. On the whole one must be careful with attempts to represent conceptually earlier stages of consciousness. Such attempts can never be completely satisfactory, because man at that time still lacked concepts. But how else are we to go about it? On the other hand, it is also more the case that myth tells us what took place at a time when historical writing did not—indeed, could not—exist. But we must be careful to approach the myths in the right way; there is much more involved than we might imagine at first sight. This is true, for example, regarding the transformation from the magical to the mythical

*Publisher's note: This and many of the following selections in Parts One and Two draw heavily on Enomiya-Lassalle's study of the work of the German thinker Jean Gebser (1905–1973).

consciousness as represented in Greek mythology. The story of Troy and Paris, the pursuit of Helen—all of this portrays man's search for the soul.

Man of archaic consciousness still experienced himself as totally one with the universe. For him, there existed no distinct other, much less the extreme dualism that still to a great extent imprisons us today. Thus, man at this stage was still without space, without time, without an ego—an unimaginable situation for us today, but there is no other way to describe it. The essence of this stage of consciousness was identity, or fusion, and in that sense totality. Both of these are lacking in modern man, and their absence is the cause of many serious problems, including the threat of nuclear war and the elusiveness of lasting world peace. If subject-object dualism could be transcended there would be no more war and the possibility of eternal peace would become very real. Nevertheless, it is not simply a matter of retreating back into the past. We must make a long detour to get to the point where we finally understand this—this time on a much deeper level.

Archaic consciousness was followed by *magical consciousness*. Man of this second stage still lacked an ego. Typical also for this stage was union with nature, a condition that we can still imagine and experience to some degree and perhaps even desire. Nevertheless, man of this structure already experienced a certain decadence, although we cannot be sure how long it took for this to make itself felt. When it did occur, the positive aspects of the magical degenerated into mere sorcery. Our modern conception of magic is perhaps more negative than positive. It is the magic of the decadent; however, originally magic was not like this.

Finally there followed *mythical consciousness*. The essence of this structure was a breakthrough to the "distinctly other" and with it the recognition of an individual ego and soul. When we speak of myths today, we usually think of something which is not true. However, myths are of great significance for what they reveal about the nature of consciousness. Nevertheless, in this stage too a certain decadence eventually set in. Although the man of earlier times also had something of religion in him, it was completely part of him. Now he became capable of projecting religion outside of himself. He could now experience the godhead as something separate. It also seems that mythical man, instead of creating a pantheon of gods, first practiced a form of monotheism. It was not until later that a world inhabited by many gods came into existence. For man of the mythical consciousness, it was still as if he were circumscribed by a circle from which he could not free himself by his own power.

That became possible only with conceptual thinking, which belongs to the next stage, that of *mental consciousness*. This process had its start in the West with the emergence of Plato's concept of the "Ideas." There was a parallel development in the East, in India, although it occurred much earlier—perhaps preceding that in the West by a thousand years or more. But it developed there differently. People in the East have adopted the new without allowing it to fall into overrationalism. The other, prerational structures survived, which led to a much healthier and more favorable situation than occurred in the West.

3

The New Integral Consciousness

In speaking of a new consciousness and attempting a historical representation of the foregoing stages of consciousness, we can talk in terms of a zero-, a one-, a two-, and a three-dimensional consciousness. Accordingly, the new consciousness can be characterized as four-dimensional. However, it would be wrong to assume that the new consciousness includes only this single fourth dimension and nothing else. If that were so, we would be incapable of representing anything in this new consciousness. Rather, the other earlier dimensions remain, although this time in more appropriate measure and not to excess. It is also incorrect to say that the new consciousness is a synthesis of the four preceding stages, for that would mean nothing basically new. Rather, the fourth dimension is of an integrating nature, raising the existing dimensions to a new and higher level. Nevertheless, the fourth dimension itself resists representation. Such representation is difficult because it is impossible to integrate the fourth dimension as long as the other dimensions exercise sole control over our consciousness.

What is meant by an aperspectival experience of reality? It is an experience of reality that goes beyond those experiences of reality found in the preceding stages of consciousness. People of the archaic, magical, mythical, and mental stages of consciousness had their own respective experiences of reality. The mythical consciousness, for example, had its own particular experience of reality. In order to clarify what we mean by an aperspectival experience of reality, we can use an example from our own experience of time.

4

Time-Freedom, Transparency, and Holistic Experience

There are three typical criteria we use to express the aperspectival world. The first criterion consists of attempts to concretize time in the sense of "time-freedom," that is, the attempt to overcome conceptual time. Here we must distinguish between eliminating time and overcoming it. Things as they stand are not to be discarded but rather overcome in order to be transcended, although they still remain. We see this situation in the arts today.

The second criterion is *transparency*, which penetrates through concepts and words to the very essence of things and which is not the result of rational deduction. When we want to understand the essence of things it is our habit to think about them: we take things apart or "analyze" and seek the grounds of their existence. Such methods may bring a partial understanding of the essence of things. However, transparency does not mean the elimination of thinking, concepts, and words; it is more a matter of going through the concepts and words to the essence underlying them. Perhaps this is the right place to speak about something that many who have practiced Zen under my direction have related and that I myself experience every day as a priest during prayer. One reads every word and every syllable with full attention, understanding the meaning without further reflection. It is only then that one can experience what exists *beyond* the words. One can learn to do this through meditation, although it usually requires a long period of application. When reading, one should take care not to read too fast, though once again it is necessary to avoid reading too slowly. In so doing, one eventually "sees through" the words to the essence underlying them, even though it remains impossible to express this in words. Although this is only one example, it is something generally valid. Here we have transparency that does not depend on rational deduction but rather penetrates through to the essence underlying the concepts and words.

The third criterion is *holistic experience,* which is to be constantly aware of the whole and thereby overcome the more extreme forms of dualism. To become capable of perceiving the whole is not something that happens overnight. But when we reach this stage and then take a further step, becoming aware also of the religious element, we have overcome dualism. Then it is no longer a matter of either-or. It is actually this dualism that makes our lot worse than that of the animals. There are many instances of one-to-one combat in the animal world, but in most cases such fights among members of the same species do not end in death. As soon as one creature realizes that it is losing, it retreats and the other allows it to go. This is something we have obviously forgotten on the path of evolution from animal to human being.

5

Transparency, or The Current Exigency as a Symptom of the Crisis

I wish to speak once again about transparency, which is something we cannot bring about just by wishing for it. Then what can we do? The answer could be: Avoid preconceived opinions while renouncing extravagant desires and blindly ruling demands. Jean Gebser tells us that only when egoism is overcome can we achieve a harmony among all the components and structures of consciousness inherent in us and thus become capable of transparency and awareness of the whole. The reason for our current exigency does not necessarily lie in the oppression and distress we see around us—for example, in the fact that millions of people are dying from hunger. These are serious matters, but they are only symptoms. Even if we were to eliminate these symptoms it would not mean that the new consciousness would manifest itself. We respond, of course, to these symptoms and seek remedies, but at the same time we must realize that the new consciousness will not break through solely as the result of these remedies. Many people say that they would like somehow to help bring the new consciousness into being. These same people sometimes chastise themselves for being unable to respond adequately to the hungry children of the world. Nevertheless, meditation is not a waste of time. For when we are more peaceful and centered in our own being, we can use our time more wisely and to the best avail for our brothers and sisters.

6

What Can and Should Be Done?

Here another question arises. What can and should we do so that the new consciousness will break through? Only a few general guidelines will be given here. Concrete and detailed directions will follow later.

First and foremost, we must strive to overcome the sole validity of rational thinking. In other words, it is a matter of not allowing ourselves to be forced by the three-dimensional into this or that system. When we are able to do this, the mental-rational will change from being the central component to become only one component along with the magical and mythical, which together will be integrated into diaphaneity (transparency). One possible help could be the concept of noncategorical elements or "systases," as Jean Gebser calls them, which would act to overcome the simple concept of time and make other aspects of time perceptible, thus allowing us to realize time as an ever-present fullness of a spiritual nature.

We should also remain aware that we live in a period of transition. If we want to be liberated from the affliction at which we have arrived through a consciousness where only "clock time" has any validity, we must free time from this rational violence. In this sense, we can speak about a rehabilitation of time. To bring this about is certainly no easy thing. It means transcending the logical thinking that at least in the West has seemed for two thousand years to be the ultimate and indeed for a long time has been so. It is precisely for this reason that many people still consider it impossible to be freed from this entanglement. Nevertheless, it is a fact that we have been fighting and suffering for this liberation for a long time already, even if we have not been aware of it. Until a few decades ago, it was still possible for many people to use their religious affiliations to avoid the whole problem that afflicts us today in the mental conscious sphere. An omnipotent creator, eternity, and so on were unquestioned postulates of faith for many people. The provincial man was assured in his world and so did not need to seek new assurances. There was still a collective faith that stood behind individual believers. This is no longer true today, at least not among people in the West. As is well known, the foundations of religion have been severely shaken by rationalism, which finally led to the declaration "God is dead."

There are still people today who manage to hold themselves above the flood despite the general crisis outlined above. But the number of those who can still do so is decreasing all the time. The conceptual representation of religious truths is no longer sufficient even for upright Christians. Many of these people no longer look to theology for their healing; they turn rather to different ways of experiencing God for themselves. This is a typical phenomenon of our time and should not be seen as a loss. Actually, it is a step forward. Besides, the mental has never been able to grasp the mythical, not to mention the magical. By limiting ourselves to the mental we affirm perhaps only a third of the world's reality, a fact that should be obvious from the earlier discussions about the structures of consciousness.

The new structure should integrate everything. However, because it cannot be systematically understood there is mistrust and fear among many people who are still imprisoned in the rational. In answer to such misgivings it must be acknowledged once more that everything that has been said and could still be said about the new consciousness should not be understood as indisputable or irrefutable. These are only cautious, if not totally unfounded, conjectures. We shall have certainty about these things only when the new structure has been integrated. It is similar to the previous transitions from one structure of consciousness to the next. Much less can we imagine now concretely and in all its details, how life in the world will be. The only thing we can do is attempt to identify the first manifestations of the new mutation.

7

The Hour of Birth for the New Man

Many phenomena of our time that are uncomfortable and give cause for worry can be considered to be the birth pangs of the new man. Humanity as a whole suffers during this birth process, like a woman who brings a child into the world. For people born in an earlier time, much of this may seem to be contrary to common sense. They believe and hope perhaps that everything is a temporary crisis to be endured and that sooner or later man will find his way back to the old ways and all present symptoms will be eradicated, like a debilitating disease which will finally be healed after all.

People of greater insight know, to the contrary, that there can be no return to the old times and that it is senseless to try to turn back the wheel of evolution. They know that what matters most is that this new man come into the world healthy and vigorous. No matter how many proximate and immediate causes one may attribute to this development, in the final analysis they are all accidental causes. The actual cause is the nature of the new human being, who is so constructed that the hour of his birth must come sooner or later. For it is personality, "being a person," that is the inmost core of the human being, and the more aware we are of this, the more human we are.

This, however, implies a longing and demand for greater personal freedom, a demand that is unmistakable among the younger generation. When this relationship is known, we can understand why such demands should not be casually dismissed as mere disobedience or insubordination. It is only natural that the new man has questions about many things and wishes to make his voice heard regarding decisions that concern him as an individual. Anyone who can do so without difficulty, however, thereby demonstrates that he has not yet participated in this newest development of the human being. Such a person belongs to a time which is already past. On the other hand, there is a danger that justifiable claims will be made in such a way that they disregard the claims of our neighbors to that same freedom. But that would be to contradict their own spirit.

8

A New Way of Thinking and a New Uprightness

We must also be capable of seeing things clearly in addition to being upright; these two qualities are in an inseparable relationship with each other. In understanding this challenge, we must examine a few other points. There are two matters in particular that pose a continual threat to interpersonal relationships and that must be overcome before we can hope to improve these relationships with the help of any system.

The first is that we are almost always blinded in our thinking by prejudices of one sort or another. There is hardly a person around who can think totally free of prejudice. The second is that hardly anyone exists who is truly sincere and, it must be added, who is at all capable of being so, even though he may wish to be so and even perhaps believes he is. The sole exception here is presented by children, to the extent that they have not been contaminated by their elders. Anyone who doesn't believe this should ask himself, after he has said or done something, why he said or did this rather than something else. Then he will often confirm for himself that what he said was not the truth but rather a colored version of it. The result is that hardly anyone trusts anyone else; we are always worried about being cheated. So long as this situation remains, the trust that is necessary for human beings to live together happily will be impossible. In addition, no true love can exist among men—although love is the most precious gift of heaven, without which no system can make humanity happy. For as the Gospels say, "there is no fear in love." (I John 4:17).

We must look these facts straight in the eye. If the new man is really to be an improvement over the old (and that he must be, otherwise he won't be new), he must be capable of sincerity and unbiased thinking. Everyone comes into the world with a particular set of hereditary factors, although education and many other things act to form that person into the completely unique, one-of-a-kind person that he or she is. Much of what the person acquires himself is good, but everything inevitably tends toward the acquisition of fixed conceptions and habits. One's unpleasant experiences and disappointments make a particular contribution here. Taken together, they act like a tinted glass that makes everything appear a certain color. Thus over the years one acquires many biases that consciously or unconsciously influence one's judgment. But this prevents the operation of the new way of thinking that the new human being is to carry out. Our age, more than any other time, is pushing toward a new way of thinking. It is a violent change that will bring into question much of what up to now has seemed to be a matter of course. At work in this drive is a longing for truth and reality.

9

The Forerunners, Tauler and Eckhart: Returning to Mysticism

The new thinking must be "mystical thinking," that is, a thinking that is free from all disorganized limitations, something that is possible only after a long process of purification.

Now one may ask: If a person matures, learns, has experiences, and thus develops his views and goes on his way conscientiously and unselfishly according to those views, isn't this simply that particular person's way? How could he do otherwise? That at least is the current conception in the West. In the East it has never been totally like this. The East has not yet forgotten that, in addition to the knowledge gained through the senses and understanding, there is another form of understanding, which Karl Albrecht calls "mystical understanding." It was Albrecht, too, who formulated the previously mentioned theory of "mystical thinking." In the West, this consciousness has been lost, with the exception of isolated cases such as the mystics. Tauler expresses himself clearly on this point when he says that a person who has arrived at this understanding "knows in a moment what he should do, where he should ask and what he should preach about." Theodor Steinbüchel says of Meister Eckhart:

> [Eckhart] the mystic, in his totally concrete ethos of the world and of Man, speaks about the "moment"—one is reminded of Kierkegaard—when God walks before the soul as the one who demands. In the moment, "to wait for God and follow Him alone in the light that He wishes to show you, through doing and letting go, to be so free and new in each moment,

as if there were nothing else you wanted to do or could do other than what is given you and expected of you in this moment—this is the fruit of God's birth." Who will not be astonished to find, in a mystic from whom one expects rapture and ecstasy, such immediacy, such freedom from all predisposed practices? Together with the ethic of principles from the Scholastics, which he knew and acknowledged, Meister Eckhart the mystic combines the concrete situation ethic. How near he is to us. [*Mensch und Gott in Frömmigkeit und Ethos der deutschen Mystik,* Düsseldorf, 1952, p. 225]

According to this, mystical knowing, which we are used to seeing as unclear and uncertain, is actually more reliable than deductive knowing.

The question concerning the new man is whether what was once the exception can now become the rule. Is it not precisely mystical knowing, free as it is from all prejudice, that is crucial in order to realize the true essence of things? It is at least true that unbiased thinking affords more hope of embracing the truth in its purity. If evolution should move in this direction, perhaps the necessary conditions will be created for man to be upright and he will then become so.

This connection becomes particularly clear when one learns how to arrive at this kind of thinking. To actually become free from all biases, the entire spirit must undergo a purification process. The more this purification process goes forward, the more free and unattached we shall be within. At the same time, this has the effect of eliminating fear and all the other unregulated motives that can lure us to dishonesty. There would no longer be any reason to avoid telling the truth. *Nemo gratis mendax*—no one lies without reason. Anyone who is free within can no longer lie. The single exception might be when we wished to help our neighbor or shield him from harm.

PART TWO

THE DIMENSIONS OF COSMIC CONSCIOUSNESS

God's existence can never be demonstrated logically or scientifically. Overemphasis on the rational has led us to view science as omnipotent, but this has also become problematical for us. Young people today seek experience, not memorized proofs for God's existence. On the path of experience that leads toward intimacy with God and unity with Him, toward absolute truth, the seeker undergoes a transformation of consciousness that possesses mystical qualities.

The mere possibility of experiencing a fourth dimension is a source of hope and strength for many people. Through this experience, man becomes transparent and perfected for the presence of God. "Perfection consists not in knowledge but rather in the force with which we are seized" (Thomas Aquinas).

The ego is a great obstacle on the way to our true self and to a deep recognition of the nature of our true existence. However, with an increasingly integral consciousness, we attain freedom from ego and are allowed entry into the divine source residing in the soul. This new consciousness is an experience of the present, of the here-and-now without looking back to the past or forward to the future. As many Zen masters say, "What was true yesterday is no longer true today." In Matthew 6:34 we read: "Take therefore no thought for the morrow: for the morrow shall take thought for the things of itself. Sufficient unto the day is the evil thereof."

A person who has prevailed over time and space suddenly finds himself with the time and the strength of will to avoid those illnesses that have their origin in our modern condition of being constantly pressed for time. Nevertheless, representation of the fourth dimension remains a central problem. Great artists like Picasso have made attempts visually to anticipate what is to come, but it was Albert Einstein who introduced the term "fourth dimension." Although first used in the field of physics, the expression has since found its way into various other areas, including references to a mutation of consciousness. Einstein's formulation of the theory of relativity transformed the prevailing static view of the universe into a new space-time continuum. By transcending opposites and dualism, the new man finds his way to freedom from space and time.

If we become capable of changing our vantage point, we possess a more varied perspective and thus free ourselves for more open thinking and for the higher stages of consciousness. Only with a new consciousness can the problems attendant to our economic advances be steered in a positive direction. If dualism and opposites cease to exist, the necessity for war will also be eliminated. We will then be ready for a permanently peaceful life together. If East and West can come closer to each other, if discoveries and experiences can be exchanged in an atmosphere of mutual tolerance and understanding, the way will open to a more hopeful future, in which the avenues of East and West will no longer be one-way streets. In this light, Enomiya-Lassalle appraises the role of Teilhard de Char-

din in helping us to a realization of the cosmic in man. As Teilhard writes:

> *To perceive cosmic energy "at the fount" we must, if there is a* within *of things, go down into the internal or radial zone of spiritual attractions. Love in all its subtleties is nothing more, and nothing less, than the more or less direct trace marked on the heart of the element by the physical convergence of the universe upon itself.*

[The Phenomenon of Man, *London, 1959, p. 265*]

10

Mystical Experience and Scientific Discovery

Beyond a doubt there is mystical as well as scientific knowledge. There have been times in the past when mystical or meditative knowledge was cherished more than scientific knowledge, a much more recent arrival. Over time, this situation has changed in favor of science. In the last few centuries, the knowledge gained by scientific discovery reached such an apex of recognition that it exercised almost sole dominion, at least in the eyes of a large number of people. In contrast, the mystical knowledge gained in meditation almost ceased to have any value of its own. As recently as thirty years ago, a German scientist whom I knew personally could say, "That which cannot be measured does not exist for me." All of us are familiar with the words of Descartes: *Cogito ergo sum,* "I think, therefore I am." Today such extremes in thinking have become dated. There are people today who are no longer capable of rational belief in God and only through meditative experience find their way back to God. For those who eschew anthropomorphic references to God, we can express it in terms of a return to an ultimate reality, to the Absolute.

During the recent period of exclusive emphasis on science, the common tendency was to view science as the single source of authentic knowledge and to reject religious faith as outmoded. Not all that long ago many people believed it was only a matter of time before religion disappeared of its own accord. In many countries, especially Western nations including the United States, a large number of people, perhaps the majority, took this standpoint. For a long period until quite recently, there were even people who could accept the arguments on both sides and say, "From the religious standpoint there is a God and whatever goes along with him, namely religion. From the scientific standpoint, however, there is no such thing." It is actually amazing that we, or at least many of us, were able to live with this contradiction for so long. It was possible only because there was still traditional belief or, better said, a collective religious consciousness, something that is no longer generally true. This has ceased to be the case, for example, in Europe and the United States and in parts of the East such as Japan. Yet even today there are countries, India for example, where a collective religious consciousness is still very strong. If you have ever been there you will have sensed this immediately.

However, although the general absence of a collective religious consciousness is the reason we are no longer able to "digest" this contradiction, it must be emphasized that the present situation is once again different. Science, although recognized in its own right, is no longer a viable replacement for religion in the minds of modern people. Nevertheless, people are not helped when confronted with articles of faith or proofs for God's existence. Today we take it for granted that such approaches are of little worth. However, in my youth—which is to say, quite some time ago—it was still possible to make a start of sorts with such articles of faith. Though they could never be a substitute for actual belief, they were nevertheless an aid. Were we to try today to prove the existence of God to a young person, such attempts would be doomed to failure—and not a little boring for the listener. . . .

In the meantime, a great longing for religious experience has awakened. And in response to this, there is intense interest in meditation, including Zen meditation with its goal of realizing the truth for oneself. All of this is directly linked to the arising of a new consciousness and the transformation of human consciousness occuring in our time. We must make at least an initial attempt to clarify the meaning of this transformation of consciousness and the extent to which these are already manifestations of the aperspectival world. It is a transformation that is taking place throughout humanity and has nothing to do with the very natural changes in individual consciousness that take place in our lives from childhood to adulthood. And although the transformation of consciousness occurs throughout humanity, not all individuals participate in it at the same time.

11

---

*The Present Crisis as a
Harbinger of the Fourth Dimension
of Consciousness*

According to Jean Gebser, there are two phases to each
structure of consciousness, the qualitative-moderate, which is
efficient and the quantitative-immoderate, which is deficient.
This might lead us to conclude that here, as elsewhere, the
new degenerates and finally collapses after a certain period of
time. This observation has been made about many religions.
In most religions the founder is a holy one who has been
called. He gains many followers, and a religion is formed. But
in the process the original spirit dies and only the forms
remain, maintained with great effort by those who survive
until a storm finally sweeps everything away.

However, on closer examination we see that this is totally
different with the consciousness structures. As a structure
becomes deficient it certainly undergoes impoverishment and
exhaustion, but also the guarantee of a new mutation. Each
mutation is a further perfection of man, a step forward in the
best sense. But at the same time there is the danger that a
structure will become immoderate as it loses its sense of limits.
This is where we find ourselves today. The solution is not
another scientific step forward, which could only mean a
further quantification, nor is it a falling back into esotericism
in the sense of occult practices. Technology also has its limits.
One needs only to reflect on the automobile, which becomes
ever more perfect and numerous, but at the same time ever

more a hindrance since both space and fuel are limited. Here, too, we find ourselves at a dead end.

In the present crisis we should not forget that, in the past, the downfall of a consciousness structure was always at the same time a sign and even a hidden guarantee of an upcoming structure. This is why it is so important that the fourth dimension be integrated. When modern man is able to gain some inkling of what is meant by this new dimension, he will be able to breathe easier. He will become aware of new strengths, since other possibilities will occur to him that he did not think of before. On the other hand, every one-sided solution is doomed a priori to failure. It is not a solution but, even in the most favorable circumstances, only a postponement. For it is temporally restricted and mental, regardless of whether it is focused on the merely measurable or the immeasurable. We are concerned here neither with an ascent nor a descent but with a transposition, a reordering, a mutational unfolding. This transposition will result in the origin's becoming visible, in a transparency, a translucence among and through man. It is proof of a new mutation through which the preceding time-space developments that presented themselves in the increasing dimensionalization of consciousness are integrated and become meaningful.

Through this transparency the present contradiction between believing and knowing, between myth and science will be surmounted. To be sure, this dualism is abolished without rational grounds. That is incomprehensible from the standpoint of the mental structure. Nevertheless, diaphaneity as it is meant here does not stand in contradiction to the rational; it transcends it.

12

Becoming a Part of the Whole through Freedom from Ego

Space and time relationships have already been described in our discussion of individual consciousness structures; now the various space-time relationships among these structures need to be elucidated further. Magical man was conscious neither of time nor space, a situation that we can no longer comprehend today, virtually possessed as we are by consciousness of space and time. Magical man did not experience the world as something distinguishable from himself, since he had not yet discovered his ego. There was nothing facing him as yet, no opposite. He was a part of a whole. A little child does not experience its environment as something foreign because it is not yet sufficiently developed as an individual. In the same way, there are moments for us all when the I-consciousness disappears, so to speak. This can occur voluntarily or involuntarily, in any of various ways. In such cases, the objective world that stands opposite us is no longer there as it usually is. And yet this situation is not the same as that of magical man, since he had not yet discovered his ego. We must distinguish here between absence of ego and freedom from ego. The former is proper to magical man, the latter to man of integral consciousness. . . .

Besides quantitative time there is also time in the qualitative sense. For example, we feel that the years go by more slowly in youth than when we are older. Or, to take another example, a minute of great pain seems longer to us than an hour of great joy.

13

Prevailing over Space and Time:
How to Cope with Stress
and Cancer

Just as there are different types of time, so there has also been
the absence of time. During the first stage of consciousness,
that of archaic man, time literally did not exist, for there was
no experience of it. Magical man of the next stage experienced
time, though in a way fundamentally different from our
present experience of it. In referring to these earlier experiences of time, Jean Gebser uses the term *Zeithaftigkeit,* or
"temporicity" [a word that attempts to express how time was
still only a quality, not yet a measurable quantity]. Magical
man was aware of day and night, and through the lunar phases
he could experience time periods longer than those experienced with the daily sun. This explains why we have twelve
months in a year.

Temporicity is not bound to space and is therefore nonquantitative. This nonquantitative time emerged out of the single-
point consciousness of magical man through the aspect of
movement. Here the point became a line, not a straight line
but a line closed in upon itself wherein man of the mythical
structure was protected or enclosed. For this reason the
symbol of the mythical period is the circle. The temporicity
characteristic of the mythical structure of consciousness cor-
responds to the psychic aspect, which was discovered during
this same period. Common to both is movement. In the
magical structure there was no space and no absence of time
in the sense that this was true for the archaic structure. In the

mythical structure there was temporicity, though not yet the distinct time phases of past, present, and future.

It is only with the advent of the mental structure that we finally encounter conceptual time, which is quantitative and thus can be referred to as "clock time." Here for the first time a sharp delineation is made between past, present, and future. Time measures and divides—in contrast to the temporality of the two earlier stages, which unites. This new form of time eventually cut the mythical view of the world into shreds. Nevertheless, in the beginning—during the first few centuries after Plato—mental consciousness was not as radical or extreme as it has become today. Nor were people in the earlier stages of mental consciousness so threatened by time as we are today. As with the other stages of consciousness, everything was good at the start until a certain decadence set in and the situation became unbearable, requiring the emergence of something new.

How is time encountered in the aperspectival experience of reality? Briefly, it is not the absence of time but freedom from time. What does freedom from time mean? It means that time is no longer a threat, which is something that will be possible once we live fully in the present moment. This condition is, or will be, typical for the new consciousness once it is fully integrated in the human psyche.

Today we still live almost exclusively in the past or future. This is the phenomenon of clock time, when you never have enough time. Typical accompanying characteristics are heart disorders, nervousness, and cancer, all of which could be called modern illnesses. Formerly, many people died of plague and cholera, diseases that we have since learned to control through prompt countermeasures. In contrast, the illnesses typical of our age occur for the most part due to stress. We may not be able to avoid stress, but we can find ways to break it down naturally without recourse to medicines or tranquilizers. If we can achieve this naturally, as is the case in meditation, stress will no longer be harmful. If we can then integrate meditation into our lives to the point where we are no longer subject to stress, all the better. This should become possible eventually, regardless of whether religious experiences occur or not. Many people say, "How can I do that? I don't have the time." To them I can only answer, "Maybe you'll find the time, when it's already too late!"

14

Prophetic Elements in the Arts

To clarify this situation, it will be helpful to consider the arts. They have played a crucial role in the development of human consciousness because ensuing stages of consciousness were first hinted at in the arts. The arts intimate a new structure of consciousness, but one that has yet fully to reveal itself. As with thought, in the arts too there was a moving forward from one dimension to another. Magical thinking was one-dimensional but then developed further. In the arts, this development reached three dimensions. In Michelangelo, for example, we already encounter a three-dimensional form of art. Nevertheless, it is always the case that the arts arrive earlier. They portray something that we do not yet know.

A similar situation exists now concerning the new consciousness. Picasso's works are representative attempts at a transformation of consciousness. Picasso wanted to depict the fourth dimension, something that by its very nature defies representation. What is the artist to do then? If he attempts to represent the fourth dimension, it can only emerge as asymmetrical. When you look at Picasso's famous portrait of a woman, it often seems as if half the face has slid halfway down the canvas. This problem of depicting the fourth dimension is common to all the contemporary arts, though it is of course important to make a distinction here between genuine art and kitsch. Nor is it by any means the case that every product of modern art is a successful representation of the fourth dimension.

In prehistoric caves, drawings have been found of quadrupeds whose four legs are lined up in a row, as if a little child had drawn them. Here we still have only two dimensions. One could say that each individual progresses through all the dimensions starting in early childhood. Nevertheless, we have yet to arrive at the fourth dimension. It is my personal opinion that when man has integrated the fourth dimension—that is, when children reach the fourth dimension in the same matter-of-fact way that they now attain to rational thinking at a certain age—humanity will have achieved enlightenment.

We can speak about other forms of art. I have already mentioned how the arts always foretell something new. Nevertheless, it is important to see to the bottom of things. In music, for example, it is not a matter of course that jazz, just because it is new, necessarily has anything to do with the fourth dimension. But, it may be the case that any experiment in this direction is still unbearable for many people—although not for many others. Such a matter is difficult to evaluate. Everything is in a state of flux.

15

The Fourth Dimension

A more detailed explanation of the fourth dimension is needed in order to gain a better understanding of its relationship with integral consciousness.

The true fourth dimension is not a dimension in the same sense as the first three. Rather, the phrase refers to time-freedom as a noncategorical element, a "non-mension," so to speak. It brings about both the dissolution and integration of the three spatial dimensions. It dissolves the measurable and passes through it. The expression "fourth dimension," which originated with Einstein, is often used today in fields other than physics. As a result, we must pay careful attention to what is meant when the fourth dimension is spoken of in another context. Our usage of the expression refers to the mutation of the consciousness that, like all previous mutations, is already present, latent in us, must burst forth, and subsequently manifests itself commensurate with its metamorphosizing power. For any realization of a fourth dimension to be "world-building," it must be seen not just as an additional dimension but as one that integrates all the others. Otherwise the result is merely a further expansion of space, which in the long run can only act to destroy the world.

It must be understood that whatever the fourth dimension implies for this mutation is different from what the fourth dimension means in physics, since this dimension of consciousness is concretely effective in all areas of life and thought. This was overcome only partially through the simple introduction of "time" (in the sense of "temporicity") to the already existing conception of space. What needs to be accomplished is a conquest of time in the sense of liberation, not simply as an expansion of space. On the other hand, three-dimensional space is not to be destroyed, any more than the two-dimensional plane was destroyed by the presence of three-dimensional space. Liberation from a world that was formerly poorer by one dimension is above all a liberation from the exclusive validity of a structure with fewer dimensions. To return to the Einsteinian fourth dimension, we can note references throughout to an all-embracing validity—for example, its invisibility, which should not be confused with abstraction. For this, too, is another area that is not conceivable with ordinary rational thinking.

Time-freedom is another aspect of the fourth dimension that by its very nature defies definition. We can understand it somewhat by answering three questions. First, what is freedom from time? It is the archaic, original "pretemporicity" in a conscious form. Archaic man did not yet have any idea of either time or "temporicity." Thus there was no lack of time for him, while we moderns are continuously pressed for time and in the resulting stress never come to rest. This does not mean that archaic man was time-free in the sense of being free of time. He was rather time-less. But because of this he lacked something that belongs to the fully evolved human being. When we today become aware of this perfect state of being, unaffected by any form of time while remaining aware of all its forms, we are able to enjoy them all without being oppressed by them in any way. Time-freedom is neither timelessness nor temporicity and yet it is still time.

The second question is: To what extent is time-freedom realizable? We realize it when we understand the nature of these individual structures—magical timelessness, mythical temporicity and mental conceptual time—in their effective character as a totality and live them in accordance with the appropriate level of consciousness. This concretion of time is what makes us open to preconscious proto-time-freedom; to this extent conscious time-freedom is the quintessence of all time forms that have existed up to now. Becoming aware of all three forms of time is at the same time liberation from all three. Everything becomes present and hence a present that can be integrated. This means also that the origin that was known beforehand becomes present. Then we perceive the ground of the world and are no longer exclusively bound to the experience-and-idea forms of the world. We no longer see the world as being fixed perspectivally. It is now aperspectival and unfixed. Anyone who has succeeded in realizing and thereby concretizing the three forms of time so basic up to now—that is, magical time-freedom, mythical temporicity, and mental conceptual time—stands in fourth-dimensionality and is aware of it.

The third question is: Why is time-freedom the fourth dimension? Because it constitutes and contains the fourth dimension. Through time-freedom the foundations will become transparent right up to the original and preconscious pretemporicity. As the conscious form of pretemporality, time-freedom is thus the fourth dimension. We must remember that it is impossible to actually represent the fourth dimension and everything that goes along with it. Thus the explanation above, which is based on Jean Gebser's work, will be unsatisfactory for many people. But it is simply an attempt that may serve as a start at understanding. Only one who has integrated the fourth dimension knows what it is, and for that person it is a matter of course.

16

The Theory of Relativity, or Prevailing Over Materialism

In discussing manifestations of the aperspectival world, we must cite at the outset the field of physics. Although I have been occupied with Jean Gebser's writings for quite some time, only recently have I become acquainted with the works of Fritjof Capra. In the process, I have discovered that Capra's book *The Tao of Physics* (1975) is an excellent complement to Gebser's works. Capra actually quotes Gebser quite often. However, there is an additional element in Capra's books to which Gebser does not formally address himself, and which is directly related to the new physics. One thing is certain. If you wish to get any sort of general grasp on the spiritual world situation, you can no longer ignore the latest developments in physics.

Here let me quote the noted German physicist Carl-Friedrich von Weizsäcker, from his book *Zum Weltbild der Physik* (1945):

> The mechanical worldview of classical physics that was valid up to 1900 has been more thoroughly destroyed than one would have expected. This is not a misfortune but rather a good lesson . . . . The new physics is the first self-contained system of knowledge about nature comprehensible in exact mathematical terms beyond the confines of the mechanistic worldview." [Cited in Gebser, *The Ever-Present Origin*, p. 370]

"Mechanistic worldview" is an indirect reference to a conception of the natural world that dominated until very recently, one that still portrays the totality in terms of interactions among inanimate material particles. Here it is only natural to mention Einstein, the discoverer of the fourth dimension. Central also to physics is the nature of time. Through Einstein's discoveries, time was freed from simple abstraction to become a relative element in our view of the universe, a view that no longer presupposes the universe to be static. The universe has become dynamic through its transformation into a newly conceived space-time continuum. The decisive step occurred with Planck's quantum theory, which demonstrated that nature actually makes leaps. Nature was not as we had been taught; no longer was it a case of everything having a cause and an effect. Such assumptions are no longer valid, for things today have become radically different. Our universe comes into being not continuously, but discontinuously in unpredictable leaps. According to this, time, rather than being a linear, continuous measure, is an intensity of a certain kind. This brings home to us the complexity of what has been hidden behind the simple concept "time."

The theory of relativity teaches that we can come to generally valid insights only when we cease to view events by analyzing them into spatial and temporal coordinates. The new physics contains yet another indication of a new approach to time when it posits the view that the world is finite yet without limits. Among other things, these various new discoveries state concretely that there is no such thing as matter since all matter can be transformed into energy.

Of course, many people are still materialists, practically speaking, but they are on a totally wrong track. What they believe is no longer true. With the new physics and many other new developments making their appearance, we are gaining new, more solid ground. Teilhard de Chardin, too, was firmly convinced that evolution never goes backward. We always move forward toward a point of perfection, toward what he called the Omega point. Even when it may be very difficult along the way, we are always moving forward and cannot go backward. Therefore, we should not be afraid of these new things making their appearance. The situation can only get better.

Nevertheless, this transformation of consciousness will certainly demand much of us. Diametrically opposed dualities such as space and time, energy and matter, the objective world and the observing subject (this last the most important pair of all) can no longer be separated. What this means is: thinking that objectifies is no longer possible. Even as we, the observers, observe the object, something is changing in that very moment. This cannot be rationally understood or represented, but it is a fact that many scientists have labored long on the matter before eventually coming to this conclusion. Werner Heisenberg, one of the most important of them, has the following to say somewhere in his writings: "It shouldn't be so, it shouldn't be possible, and yet it is."

The old diametrically opposed dualities such as subject-object, and hence the perspective of the mental consciousness, are already obsolete from the standpoint of modern physics. In addition, the dialectic of thesis-antithesis-synthesis, with which we have operated for so long, is no longer tenable. These are natural manifestations of a new consciousness, which we have termed the aperspectival. The prevailing physical view of the world is characterized by the fact that the objects of scientific observation are resistant to observation.

All attempts to represent the structural operations within the atom have been failures. Furthermore, the latest trailblazing discoveries are no accident. They have been possible only to the extent that they allow for the realization of a general readiness for a more intense structure of consciousness. The sum of all possible events creates a four-dimensional world that cannot be conceptually grasped. Although this resistance to conception seems nonrational, it will nonetheless be transformed into transparency, which is another aspect of the four-dimensional structure. The mechanical view of the world is no longer correct. Rational thinking is no longer enough. This is a total revolution in thinking. When we were young, we were often told, "You don't understand it now, but later on you will." This is not so, and as a result everything collapses. Things can only be understood through a new view of the world, through a new consciousness. Now we can grasp things only according to the prevailing consciousness, just as a child can understand only to the degree that he or she has matured. Yet nothing is lost in this process; quite the contrary. There is nothing to be afraid of. Of course, people who are responsible for education in the schools and universities may at first feel trepidation. Nevertheless, this is not something which is going to happen overnight. We have to view things positively and remain aware of what is happening.

17

Transcending Dualism in the Field of Biology

Our present understanding of rhythmic and evolutionary processes in biological events already stands on uncertain ground. Discontinuous acts can no longer be ignored. Time, once considered a quantity, now takes on the character of a quality. It is being transformed from an "ex-tensive," measurable dimension into a more "in-tensive" element with effects that cannot be determined in advance. There is even proof now of organ development free of any particular goal.

Everything we call upon as precedent with the whole of our logic and rationality has come into question. The dualisms of organic-inorganic, body-soul, matter-spirit have been overcome. Here we speak in terms of "overcoming," and the choice of words is very important. For this is not the same as doing away with these things. It must never be a matter of trying to eliminate the fundamental concept undergoing mutation but rather a matter of divesting it of its exclusiveness. In other words, it is a reaching beyond, a transcending, which is not the same thing as eliminating. It is also not true that dualism is replaced by polarity; rather it is supplanted by the principle of integration or time-freedom. Physics and biology alike have abandoned the exclusive validity of the mental by integrating magical and mythical concepts. Only a three-way harmonization among the vital, mythical, and mental aspects makes possible that leap into the fourth dimension which is characteristic of the new consciousness structure. This freedom from time and space is neither magical-vital nor mythical-psychic nor mental-rational; it is spiritual. The fourth dimension in its entirety is the first expression of a concretion of spirit. For this reason, it is also not intelligible in terms of conceptual systems, though it is nonetheless perceptible in its totality.

18

Open Thinking, or
The End of Philosophy

We come now to philosophy, which began in the West with the Greeks. The mutation from mythical to mental consciousness reached completion in the West through Greek philosophy. In all deference to the great achievements of philosophy during the twenty-five hundred years of its development, we must nevertheless state that philosophy in the conventional sense of the word has reached its end.

I recall a famous interview with Martin Heidegger. The German news magazine *Der Spiegel* requested an interview with the noted German philosopher, who agreed on condition that the contents would be published only after his death.

Toward the end of the interview, the conversation turned to philosophy, to which Heidegger remarked laconically, "Philosophy has come to an end." The interviewer protested, saying, "That can't be possible, Herr Professor. You yourself are a philosopher." But Heidegger held fast to his position; he had seen into philosophy's future. You can find similar statements in his writings.

Kierkegaard had already related the chronological moment to eternity and introduced the concept of temporality. He was followed by Henri Bergson, whose work *Time and Freedom* (1889) took up the analysis of time. According to Bergson, "Time is invention or it is nothing at all." Thus time is freed from space and attains that independence that could never have been reached by purely logical deduction. All these developments are manifestations of the aperspectival.

The mechanistic worldview is no longer tenable, and rational thinking no longer suffices. We must open ourselves up to the new, to a higher stage of consciousness in which thinking is open, no longer closed in upon itself or tied to a single perspective.

19

The New Consciousness and Unconscious Archetypes, or Avoiding Atomic War

I wish to make a few additional remarks concerning sociology. Here we can cite the French Revolution, which constituted a totally new direction in world development. Nevertheless, ensuing events failed to live up to its original promise. Today, as perhaps was possible then, we are on the verge of transcending national boundaries. And yet at the same time, we are not entirely certain whether we can avoid a third world war, one that would involve atomic weapons. We hope we can. A simple error can set the world in flames: this too would be the result of our great advances in science.

Perhaps the new consciousness must announce its arrival before we can be completely certain of our own survival. I have read Fritjof Capra's *Turning Point* with great interest, and am convinced of the essential truth of what he says. He cites experts from various fields, such as medicine, and it is a thoroughly well-founded work; however, as long as some aspect of the new consciousness fails to appear, it remains doubtful whether we will be able to actually implement what he says and not just content ourselves with theoretical understanding. Incidentally, any implementation of Capra's ideas would require great sacrifices at times. Those with many possessions would have to renounce their luxuries, as would the industries that manufacture luxury items. This is why it is so important to integrate this consciousness as much as possible in concrete ways. I am firmly convinced that this process will continue. Already we are further along the way then we were ten or twenty years ago, not to mention fifty years ago. The work goes on, and when we work in this direction we act on behalf of all humanity.

Psychology can help us here. Research on the unconscious as an aspect of the fourth dimension became a general theme in the work of Freud and Jung. Here it is not necessary to go into details. Jung expressed it in terms of archetypes that form primal patterns without possessing any material existence of their own. They are the time-free and nonmaterial bases of the psyche that nevertheless cannot be grasped with the intellect. For this reason, they transcend both simple rationality and simple irrationality. The archetypes are something that has always been there and always will be there. They are primordial images residing in the psyche whose existence is supported by dreams, fantasies, myths, fairy tales, poems, and other psychically conditioned manifestations. They themselves are, so to speak, "eternally present," which means they are free from time.

20

Teilhard de Chardin: Eastern Roads, Western Roads

Teilhard de Chardin brought together characteristics and talents seldom found in one person. He addressed the subject of evolution not only from the standpoint of natural science but also from that of philosophy, theology, and his own religious experiences. . . .

Teilhard attempts to show the reality of this convergence in the three fields of physics, metaphysics (philosophy), and mysticism. As is well known, this basic idea is expressed by Teilhard throughout his works. In his opinion the whole of evolution moves from its start toward a particular point that he calls "Omega." By this he understands

> an ultimate and self-subsistent pole of consciousness, so involved in the world as to be able to gather into itself, by union, the cosmic elements that have been brought by technical arrangements to the extreme limit of their centration—and yet, by reason of its supra-evolutive (that is to say, transcendent) nature, enabled to be immune from that fatal regression which is, structurally, a threat to every edifice whose stuff exists in space and time. [*Toward the Future*, trans. René Hague, New York, 1975, p. 185]

The Omega point for Teilhard is the "universal Christ," the Christ of the Parousia who, according to Christian belief, will come again at the end of the world. In his opinion, the universal Christ has already become visible in the fields of physics and metaphysics. One may be tempted to say that such a view could only have validity for Christians. But this would not be fair to Teilhard. The train of his thinking runs in the opposite direction. In other words, he approaches the issue of evolution not from a theological perspective but from the understanding that he gained through years of scientific research. And thereby in both physics and metaphysics he happens upon a particular situation, an evolutionary stage, at which point what is implied by the words *universal Christ* lights up spontaneously like a fulfillment.

Here it is naturally impossible to attempt a detailed discussion of what all this has to do with physics and metaphysics. But in regard to the third area, that of mysticism, what Teilhard says about the difference between the "Eastern road" and the "Western road" does need to be rectified. Teilhard maintains that only the Western form, by which he means Christian mysticism, is valid for achieving a convergence in this area. In his estimation, the road of the East is not suited for this, since mystical unity in that tradition appears and is acquired by direct suppression of the multiple. He refers to this with expressions such as "pantheism of identification," "the spirit of 'release of tension,' " and "unification by co-extension with the sphere through dissolution." He goes on to say that

> in contrast, by the very nature of the second way (the way of the West) it is impossible to become one with the whole without driving forwards the scattered elements which compose us and surround us immediately in the direction of differentiation and convergence until the end of themselves. From this standpoint, the "common basis" of the Eastern way is simply an illusion.   [*Toward the Future*, pp. 200–201]

He calls this a "pantheism of union" (and, consequently, of love), a "spirit of 'tension', unification by concentration and hyper-centration at the center of the sphere." Let us note that here too Teilhard is not concerned with a theological appraisal of Buddhism or any other non-Christian religion.

It remains a widespread notion that Eastern methods of meditation such as Yoga and Zen consider the phenomenal world (if they consider this world real at all) to be a hindrance to the experience of the ultimate reality and thus seek to suppress it. Even if this is true for certain schools, it is definitely not true for all of them. It is most certainly not true for . . . Zen meditation. The Zen masters emphasize strongly that nothing is to be suppressed in Zen. According to their teachings, the phenomenal world is every bit as real as the absolute. They are simply two aspects of the same thing. It is doubtful whether Teilhard de Chardin had much familiarity with Zen. He does not appear to have done any particular research in Japan; his scientific attention was concentrated solely on China. Besides, there was very little knowledge of Zen in Europe at that time, much less any actual Zen practice.

PART THREE

THE TRANSFORMATION OF RELIGIOUS CONSCIOUSNESS

Today we are aware of a profound transformation all around us of human consciousness, whether it is one that is religious in nature or initially purely psychological in nature. Ever since the arrival of the drug culture, altered states of consciousness have been the object of personal experimentation and empirical study. Along with these developments, various forms of meditation, including autogenic training, yoga, Transcendental Meditation and Zen, have become increasingly significant. Man is in search of himself, though he has had to make several detours and undergo much suffering in the process. It is actually natural, as part of the general process of transformation, that the religious consciousness is also being formulated in new and different ways. Existing structures of the Christian Church in the West have now come under question and are the object of much reflection. "The question is whether increasing knowledge will prove this common element to go even deeper than appeared at first, despite the differences that still remain" (Karl Jaspers).

Can we avoid a catastrophe, or will the words of Revelation soon become reality? If we continue on as we have been, may we not run up against our own destruction? Only with a further intensification of consciousness, lead-

ing to the overcoming of dualism, can we survive the present crisis.

Today, more than ever before, we are aware of a serious conflict between the older and younger generations, particularly in the area of religion. Nevertheless, by following a path usually marked by painful detours, many have found the way back to their religious roots through meditation. Scriptural passages suddenly take on new meaning as we gain access to their true message through religious experience.

The wisdom and spirituality of the East have opened up new ways to encounter God within ourselves. It is no longer the rationality of the mental intelligence that is to dominate but a consciousness filled with the spirit. Enomiya-Lasalle acknowledges his predecessor Sri Aurobindo as a bridge-builder between East and West.

21

The Transformation of Consciousness

When the discussion turns nowadays to the transformation of consciousness, most people imagine a change in individual consciousness. But there also seems to be a transformation of consciousness occurring throughout humanity, and this is one that will have a profound influence on the religious sphere regardless of individual actions. In order to clarify this phenomenon, it is appropriate here to outline what is meant by a transformation of consciousness, because the term can have many meanings.

Needless to say, concrete changes do occur in the individual consciousness, and, as past events have shown, these can also affect humanity as a whole. The entire history of human consciousness, from the first glimmers of intelligent awareness up to the present, has been an extremely complicated process. Nevertheless, we can distinguish various stages that are reflected in religious developments. We have already discussed this point elsewhere in relation to Jean Gebser's work *The Ever-Present Origin;* thus we shall limit ourselves here to the prevailing stage of consciousness, which can be termed the mental consciousness.

The stage of consciousness that dominates today began in the West about the time of Plato, that is, in connection with his concept of the "Ideas" as the basic cosmic principle. The influence of this particular consciousness has increased steadily since then, to the extent that it now all but supplants the earlier stages of consciousness in the West. It continues to dominate in Europe, America, and parts of Asia. Characteristic of this consciousness is conceptual thinking, to which we are all indebted for the great achievements in science and technology. It can be added that the influence of this "mental" consciousness has always been much stronger in the West than in the Orient. Anyone with even an elementary knowledge of those two areas of the globe will have noticed that the mental influence on the religious sphere decreases the further East one travels. Of all the religions, it is Christianty upon which mental consciousness had the greatest effect. This is because Christianity originated at the precise historical moment when this consciousness, especially as formulated in Greek philosophy, had fully established itself. Philosophy in the traditional sense was and is possible only within mental consciousness. The wide-reaching effects of this consciousness were expedited by the fact that most of Europe was united for several centuries under the Roman empire. Christian theology as we know it today also developed during this period, and it too was first made possible within the framework of this consciousness.

Since religious consciousness changes in accordance with the prevailing general consciousness, the effects of any form of meditation, such as Zen meditation, are also bound to the limits of the prevailing general consciousness. Nevertheless, if the prevailing consciousness is in a state of flux, meditation can either encourage or hinder this development, depending on the type of meditation it is. However, no form of meditation can by itself bring a new overall consciousness into being. The predisposition toward a new stage of consciousness already exists in a way that, rather than developing gradually, the new consciousness comes to sudden awakening. But we cannot will this into being. Considering history's past achievements, it is perhaps difficult for modern man to recognize his limitations in this regard. Nevertheless, particularly in the case of a transformation of consciousness, there is no Archimedean point from which the world can be totally revolutionized. On the other hand, the total process by which one transformation in consciousness follows upon another is not a matter of blind fate, since it is always directed toward the goal of a more perfect humanity.

22

Transformations in Consciousness in Karl Jaspers' "Axial Period"

The fact that great religious transformations began to take place at the beginning of the mental structure of consciousness has also been emphasized by the philosopher Karl Jaspers. His concept of an "axial period" refers to the simultaneous spiritual breakthrough from myth to reflection that occurred between 800 and 200 B.C., with its apex around 500 B.C., when the Buddha, Confucius, Lao-tzu, the Greek philosophers, and the prophets of Israel were all active. Jaspers develops this idea in his book *The Origin and Goal of History* (trans. Michael Bullock, London, 1953).

As he explains in that work, in several parts of the world there occurred simultaneously, although quite independently, an extraordinary spiritual breakthrough. In this connection Jaspers quotes the nineteenth-century German historian Ernst von Lasaulx:

> It cannot possibly be an accident that, six hundred years before Christ, Zarathustra in Persia, Gautama Buddha in India, Confucius in China, the prophets in Israel, King Numa in Rome and the first philosophers—Ionians, Dorians, Eleatics—in Hellas, all made their appearance pretty well simultaneously as reformers of the national religion. [p. 8]

In answer to the objection that these events only seem to have something in common, Jaspers takes the following position:

What is involved in the Axial Period is precisely the common element in an overall historical picture, the breakthrough to the principles which, right up to our own time, have been operative for humanity in borderline situations. The essential thing here is this common element, which does not stem from all over the earth, wherever man as such exists, but historically speaking solely from these three origins and the narrow area they occupy. The question is whether increasing knowledge will prove this common element to go even deeper than appeared at first, despite the differences that still remain. In that event, the temporal coincidence would become a fact, all the more astonishing the more clearly it is visualized.   [p. 9]

Particularly interesting is what Jaspers says in reply to the idea that these parallels have no historical character, where "history" implies causal continuity:

It is precisely this series of stages from China to Greece whose reality we deny; there is no such series, either in time or in meaning. The true situation was rather one of contemporaneous, side by side existence without contact. To begin with, several roads seem to lead from disparate origins toward the same goal. There is a multiplicity of the same in three shapes. There are three independent roots of one history, which later— after isolated and interrupted contacts, finally only a few centuries ago and properly speaking not until our own day—became a single unity.   [pp. 10–11]

Finally Jaspers comes to the following conclusion:

It seems to me continually more unlikely that this overall aspect of the Axial Period should be no more than an illusion created by historical coincidence. It seems rather to be the manifestation of some profound common element, the one primal source of humanity.

What followed later in the course of increasing diver-
gence produces occasional analogies, marks of a common origin, but never again *in toto* that real, original
community of meaning.   [p. 12]

The astonishing mutuality of the three historical origins
presses Jaspers on to the question of why this occurred.

The fact that these three regions were originally unknown to each other seems, at first, to be entirely
extraneous—but it is an historical mystery which pro-
gressive research into the facts of the situation renders
increasingly great. The Axial Period, with its over-
whelming plenitude of spiritual creations, which has
determined all human history down to the present
day, is accompanied by the enigma of the occurrence,
in these three mutually independent regions, of an
analogous and inseparably connected process. [p. 13]

Questions about the historical origins of this development
are intensified for Jaspers by the fact that these events com-
prised an outbreak within humanity in small areas and in no
way concerned the whole of mankind. What presented itself
here was not an overall development of humanity but rather a
"singular ramified historical process." Jaspers shows that the
various attempts which have been made to account for this
outbreak are inadequate and then adds:

No one can adequately comprehend what occurred
here and became the axis of world history! The facts
of this breakthrough must be seen from all sides, their
many aspects must be fixed in the mind and their
meaning interpreted, in order to gain a provisional
conception of the Axial Period, which grows more
mysterious the more closely we examine it."   [p. 18]

Nevertheless, Jaspers defends himself against suspicions
that he is hinting about divine intervention. He would much
rather "hold the question open and leave room for possible

new starting-points in the search for knowledge, which we cannot imagine in advance at all."

Perhaps the answers to these questions are provided by Jean Gebser in his exposition of the transformations of consciousness in *The Ever-Present Origin*. The fact that this development, as Jaspers understands it, did not occur in the whole of humanity but only in a relatively small part thereof, is no argument against its being an overall transformation of consciousness. For every new structure of consciousness is not realized immediately in all of humanity. It may require long periods of time for the transformation to make its way throughout all of humanity. At any rate, the descriptions of Jaspers and Gebser seem to corroborate each other.

The question about the meaning of the Axial Period, namely about what this means for humanity, is answered by Jaspers in three points that can only be mentioned here briefly: (a) If we can truly make the facts of the Axial Period our own, we gain something which is common to all of humanity, beyond all differences in religious belief. (b) This challenges us to engage in unrestricted communication, the possibility of which is established by the mutuality of the threefold origin. This is also a remedy against the "erroneous claim to exclusive possession of truth by any one creed," which has been the source of so much harm in the West. (c) Finally, there remains the question whether this period and its creations are to serve as the measure for everything that follows. Jaspers does not simply answer this question in the affirmative. A corresponding question phrased in terms of Gebser's theory of stages of consciousness would be as follows: "Will mental consciousness remain dominant for all time?" The allusion to a new consciousness is an attempt to answer that question.

23

The Present Threat: Nonsimultaneity in the Transformation of Consciousness

The great discoveries of the last decades were possible only against the background of the fourth dimension. We merely need to consider the release of atomic energy, not in terms of its dangers but rather as the product of a positive development in human consciousness. Even prior to discovering the fourth dimension, man had achieved great things with mental consciousness, particularly in science and technology, accomplishments that people of a magical or mythical consciousness could never imagine. Nevertheless, today we experience the decadent phase of mental consciousness, in which all achievements of a merely mental nature contain an additional "shadow" side. If development continues on its present course, we may well come to the point where humanity destroys itself. Such an occurrence is avoidable only if we become capable of shielding ourselves against this danger by a further intensification of consciousness. How does the new consciousness achieve this? It frees man from the excessive dualism of subject-object polarity and the relentless either-or of pure rationalism.

An overview of the situation shows that liberation from a consciousness structure that is poorer by one dimension resides in liberation from the exclusive validity of that structure. Today this means that we must gain freedom from the exclusive validity of rational thinking. It does not mean that rational thinking loses *all* validity. Such thinking remains, although now within defined limits. It may be incomprehensible to many, if not most, of the people of our time—at least within the Western cultural sphere—that there could be a form of thinking beyond rational thinking. And yet, we can hardly deny that thinking of a purely logical nature has brought us to a state of profound crisis and suffering. We are moving ever closer to a dead end. But in addition to objective thinking there has always been another form of thinking, at least for certain individuals.

Objective thinking is essentially limited by a horizon, even when we can repeatedly push that horizon further away from us. This is evident in the field of technology. It may be possible to design ever faster airplanes, but there will always be a limit. The new thinking will always break through the existing horizon. Of course, it will never be possible, even with the new form of thinking, to create airplanes of unlimited speed. Rather, the new thinking to come is a more open kind that fundamentally transcends the limits of objective thinking. Koshiro Tamaki, Professor Emeritus of Tokyo University, calls this "totally personal thinking." Such thinking is not determined solely by reason; in it intelligence, feeling, will, spirit and the body play equally important roles. That is to say, it encompasses the whole of our humanity. This thinking will reveal the *Ding an sich* that presently remains concealed behind the concepts that comprise objective thinking and therefore cannot grasp the thing itself. This means that the new thinking is a holistic thinking, one not unconditionally bound to rational thinking. Such thinking *see through* what appears contradictory in rational terms and so trancends dualistic opposition.

Since the new consciousness involves "seeing through" such dualistic opposition, this new thinking can free us from situations where we would otherwise become so entangled that we could no longer see a way out. Don't many people today doubt the fate of mankind and believe that humanity will sooner or later destroy itself? Even those who try to avoid thinking about the future feel themselves burdened by this danger.

24

Finding the Way Back to Our Religious Roots

Although there have always been differences in thinking between the older and younger generations, such differences are greater and more fundamental today than they have ever been before. This is especially true concerning religious matters. Many modern people who were raised as Christians are incapable of believing what they were taught in their childhood. Nevertheless, a longing often arises within them for something they cannot put a name on yet that appears more important than anything else. And since they can no longer find it in the Christianity they once called their own, they turn to Asia to find something that will satisfy their hunger. After a long process of transformation, many of these people find their way back to their Christian roots in a way they never expected. And this time they do not lose their faith again, because it has been truly integrated. Others find what they are looking for in other religions, though the cases where this occurs with complete success are necessarily few, since it is impossible to completely shed two thousand years of Christianity (in addition to a thousand years of Judaism) bequeathed by one's ancestors. They may formally convert to a non-Christian religion but remain, albeit now negatively, bound by their relationship to Christianity—a situation that often takes the form of intense prejudice and invective against everything Christian. It requires a long, painful process to make another religion such as Buddhism truly one's own. It is noticeable that people raised in a Buddhist tradition often have fewer preconceptions about Christianity than those who have converted from Christianity to Buddhism. One often comes across Buddhist Zen masters positively disposed toward Christianity. Many of them read the Scriptures and even quote the Bible in their instructions to their students.

25

New Access to the Scriptures

Christians who practice Zen meditation for a long time often find a new appreciation of the Scriptures through an understanding that is no longer rational. This understanding does not take the form of some new interpretation that occurs to them as the result of reading or considering a scriptural text. If this were so, they would still be at the same level as before. Rather, it is a matter of reading the words with attention while at the same time seeing through them, so to speak, to the reality behind those words and concepts. The entire person is addressed here, much as in the case of "totally personal thinking," which I have mentioned earlier. The result is an understanding that cannot be expressed in words although the experience is nevertheless accompanied by an authentic and deep joy. All of the textual disharmonies resulting from the verbal content, originally a possible hindrance to understanding, are dissolved; they are no longer felt as hindrances. Such disharmonies are no longer important because the truth has been grasped directly. The Christian encounters Christ directly, which is, after all, the goal of the Church and theology alike. Nevertheless, this is not a matter of new understanding but rather an intensification of the religious knowledge one already possesses to some extent. One could say that faith comes into view.

In this form of seeing, which is also a basic element of the new consciousness, all doubt disappears as the soul penetrates its own depths to encounter all-embracing existence. Certainly there are other forms of meditation with a similar effect, that of transforming religious consciousness. But this is possible only by means of nonobjective methods; thought and reflection would block the way here. It may well be that other types of meditation that also contain a nonrational element can indirectly help one to reach this goal—as long as they are stopped at the right time and replaced with nonobjective meditation. Saint John of the Cross confirms this when he says: "The intellect must neither burden nor nourish itself with all these perceptions and pictorial visions and any other forms or ideas which may present themselves as pictures or individual cognitions."

26

The Spiritual Vacuum in the West and What the East Has to Offer

Even prior to the First World War but more so in the years afterward, interest in spiritual exercises was high. Most of these practices, such as the Spiritual Exercises of Saint Ignatius, emphasized meditation focused on an object, but other methods were also employed. The major "Houses of Devotion" built at this time in many places [in Germany] were always full. This spiritual movement was increasingly hindered by the political situation until the Second World War eventually broke out. The postwar years saw no recurrence of a religious movement on the scale that had occurred after the First World War. Young people had to a large extent lost their religious belief. Although spiritual practices in the traditional sense did continue and something of a revival took place, these never approached the earlier scale of developments. Many Houses of Devotion stood empty or were turned over to other purposes.

Then there began a slow but steady influx of Eastern forms of meditation into the West, first Yoga—primarily in the form of Hatha Yoga—and later Zen. Today the West is all but inundated by these Eastern offerings.

That Eastern meditation has found such fertile soil is not due primarily to skillful propaganda. Rather, it is the result of a religious vacuum still spreading in the consciousness of Western man. Large portions of the population have responded intuitively to this vacuum without concerning themselves with theoretical reservations about Eastern meditation, such as are sometimes voiced by proponents of a philosophy or theology that is no longer in keeping with present-day consciousness. Anyone who clings to a level of consciousness that is now outmoded effectively loses any voice or influence in the present, no matter how bitter a pill this might be to swallow.

Today many people experience thought during meditation as more a hindrance than a help on their way to God. Even proofs of God's existence do not help them along the way; they want to experience God directly. They sense that unity with God is possible only by way of personal experience. In this respect Zen, because it is not bound to any particular worldview, can also help Christians come to an experience of God without compromising their Christian faith. The general search for religious experience originates from an unreflected, direct insight into how the exclusive validity of rational thinking has reached its limits. It is because of this transformation in consciousness today that Zen and other nonobjective forms of meditation encounter a more favorable reception than the objective forms preferred in the West in the past.

Although this direct insight into the necessity of a new consciousness has become widespread, many people nevertheless have reservations about how this can fit together with traditional Christian philosophy and theology, not to mention concern about the outward forms these beliefs take. As justified as these worries may be, especially among those who have particular responsibilities in these fields, the new consciousness cannot be challenged on the grounds that it poses a threat to conventional thinking: it is a matter not of "should" or "should not" but rather of an existing fact. The new consciousness, which has always existed potentially, inevitably awakens of its own accord when its time has come. Instead of rejecting outright the possibility of such a new consciousness, those responsible for spiritual and religious development should particularly strive to grasp the present situation and then to take a positive stance toward it by asking themselves what needs to be done. With such an open attitude, solutions to problems will eventually present themselves that no one would have dared to think about earlier. This creative task will succeed to the extent that man remains true to the experience of the new consciousness in himself.

27

Sri Aurobindo: Concrete Steps in Education toward Transformation of Religious Consciousness

In 1920, soon after the founding of his ashram in Pondicherry, India, Sri Aurobindo's colleague Mira Alsfassa—better known as "the Mother"—assumed direction of the ashram. At that time Sri Aurobindo retired completely from public life until he "left the body," as it is said, in 1950. Auroville, a city for the people of the future, was not founded until 1968, eighteen years after his death, although the project had presumably long been on his mind. Its construction took place according to his ideas, and direction of the newly founded community as well as the ashram was assumed by the Mother until her death in 1973 at the age of ninety-six.

Aurobindo left his ideas behind in voluminous writings that spoke about the transformation of consciousness that must occur. . . . The ashram in Pondicherry has as its goal working toward this goal by laboring together. Thus, rather than being an abode of meditation and peace in the usual sense of an ashram, it is an "iron hammer," to use Aurobindo's own words. It is an abode of work, since every form of work or occupation can contribute to the goal. In this regard Aurobindo said that he did not want hundreds of thousands of disciples. It would be enough to have a hundred persons of integrity who desired to become tools of God, free from the drives of the small self.

By the guidelines that otherwise hold when a city is founded, many things about the origin of Auroville seem at first glance to be inefficient or even incomprehensible. But we must keep in mind the goal underlying its founding, which is to create the best possible circumstances for the new consciousness to arise.

From the start there were no fixed rules or regulations. The formulation of such rules was left to the supramental consciousness, which would gradually come into effect. For this reason, every form of systematization was avoided. It was no longer the mental intelligence, but the spiritually fulfilled consciousness that would dominate in Auroville. Aurobindo himself emphasized that a new world was coming into being and that it was youth which must form it. The ideal was to be the birth of the person in spirit. Our lives were to be spiritually inspired, striving to create a body of action for a great birth and creation.

Naturally this was a risky undertaking, since there was no strict form of government or organization. In childrearing the customs of the past were to be avoided. The main emphasis would be on allowing the new consciousness to develop unhindered in the child, especially in the earlier school years. Children were to learn more by doing than by studying, and teachers were to help the child to find its own inner direction. This, of course, assumed that the teacher had learned this himself. In addition to the traditional areas of education, the development of mental silence or complete stillness was to be emphasized, which would encourage increasing receptiveness to the inspirations of the spirit. As Aurobindo himself states, this influence is effective for a great number of children in a way that makes itself felt in their spontaneous actions and even in their words. Unfortunately, parents for the most part don't know what this is and do not understand what is happening with their children.

Another peculiarity of this new education is that the child is permitted to move around freely in the work areas of the ashram, where teachers are ready to give him or her answers to any questions. Yet another characteristic completely in keeping with the goal is the total absence of grades and competition. Only joy in the future and the readiness to learn uninterruptedly were to be encouraged. Education should take place spontaneously regardless of the setting, whether on a tractor, under a light bulb, or whatever. Emphasis should be on the enrichment and broadening of consciousness. Most children hardly need to be supervised. They educate themselves.

The following attitudes will help people to prepare for integration of the supramental or truly spiritual: (1) the conviction that the intellect is not capable of truly comprehending the spiritual; (2) renunciation of all striving for comfort, self-gratification, and pleasure; (3) the endeavor to find joy in everything that one does without pleasure becoming the motive of one's actions; (4) never becoming excited, worried, or nervous; (5) striving to avoid taking events on the psychic plane for what they seem to be. Also encouraged are: never complaining about another if one is not in a position to change that person according to his or her nature, and never forgetting the goal. Everything is equally important. Before eating, we should wait a few seconds and wish that the nourishment will help our realization of the great discovery. The same holds for everything else we do. Before sleeping, we should wish that the sleep may give us strength in order to take up the way to the great discovery again the next morning. Before speaking, we should wait long enough to examine our words and speak only those that are necessary, never saying anything which could be a hindrance to advancing on the Way. . . .

The life of the psyche is undying life. In contrast, spiritual consciousness means living the infinite and eternal beyond time and space. In order to lead a spiritual life all ego-fixedness must be pushed aside, for one can no longer have ego. Supramental education, therefore, should bring about not so much a development of human nature and an unfolding of its latent capabilities as a transformation of this nature, a transformation of our existence in its totality, and thus a new ascent of the human species over present-day man to man of the future, so that it may finally lead to a divine humanity on earth.

As mentioned earlier, in Aurobindo's overall conception serious consideration is given to the body and along with it to the matter of work. Anyone who visits the ashram in Pondicherry will be convinced of this point. The perfection of the body has two prerequisites: (1) awakening to a consciousness of the body and (2) awakening and nurturing its abilities to the fullest extent, that is, so totally, perfectly, and multifaceted as possible.

Tensions between the ashram and Auroville developed soon after the death of the Mother. . . . Those who have lived at Auroville up to now, and who have strived there to realize the vision of Aurobindo and the Mother, are mostly from other parts of the world, especially Europe. Chiefly young people, their present numbers are about three hundred, plus about one hundred Indians. . . .

There is also a danger that, now that its future existence is fairly secure, Auroville will lose its identity. Everyone is familiar with the continual flow of young seekers from the West traveling to India and other East Asian countries. The greater number of these young people are seekers in the true sense of the word, regardless of their outer appearance. They know there are ashrams where they can live cheaply and perhaps find what they are looking for, or where at least there is the possibility of going a bit further along the way. Auroville is well known, at least in Europe and especially in France and Germany, and has a further attraction as the "City of the Future." The fact that it includes individual groups representing different languages also offers many people the possibility of entering a community where their mother tongue is understood. It is already said that many of the young people coming to Auroville no longer hold the noble aims that the city was founded on. Nor do they know what is expected of them if they are to work together for the realization of that goal. The original conditions for acceptance into Auroville were very strict, sometimes even harsh. Whatever the present circumstances may be, it is difficult to control the admission of new occupants due to this splintering into smaller groups.

We can only hope that these difficulties will eventually be overcome and that Auroville will fulfill its mission for the betterment of humanity.

PART FOUR

MEDITATION AND THE EXPERIENCE OF GOD

Enomiya-Lasalle recognized very early the great longing among many people to rediscover the original joyful state of oneness which they can no longer find in traditional religious faith. Meditation is an important way to that goal. In his widely praised book Up from Eden *(Boston, 1986), Ken Wilber agrees:*

> *If we—you and I—are to further the evolution of mankind, and not just reap the benefit of past humanity's struggles, if we are to contribute to evolution and not merely siphon it off, if we are to help the overcoming of our self-alienation from Spirit and not merely perpetuate it, then meditation—or a similar and truly contemplative practice—becomes an absolute ethical imperative, a new categorical imperative. . . .*
>
> *[Meditation] is simply what an individual at this present stage of average-mode consciousness has to do in order to go beyond that stage in his or her own case.* [p. 321]

Through the meditation practices taught by Enomiya-Lasalle and others we are given the opportunity to return into direct contact with God. The way to that goal is not easy; in fact, it is often very arduous. Something that has been lost and buried over generations is not to be regained overnight or by way of a miracle. All beginnings are difficult, and only continual, honest effort will bring the seeker to the goal. Here it is important to distinguish clearly between those methods of meditation that have been dominant up to now and "nonobjective" meditation.

Objective meditation, which can be employed by the rational mind, might at first be considered more suitable for our present consciousness. Nevertheless, the great Christian mystics of antiquity and the Middle Ages were already familiar with a form of intensive meditation that was completely free of images and concepts. We find the following passage in the writings of Francisco de Osuña, a Spanish Franciscan of the fifteenth century:

> *You should bring your reasoning mind to stillness. Understanding of things that cannot be seen belongs to pure consciousness. We speak of pure consciousness when the spirit dwells in the highest truth without any admixture of imaginative thinking. In order to achieve this you must learn to tie down your wandering memories and ideas and thereby silence thinking.*

In this fashion, an encounter with God takes place in the ground of the soul. A well is drilled in the individual soul leading to God's fountain, the wellspring of our existence.

When Eastern and Western spirituality truly encounter each other, the way they show us can then lead Christians to a personal experience of God and Buddhists to an experience of the cosmic Absolute.

In the "dark night of the soul" Saint John of the Cross made his own painful way to the experience of God. His too was a nonobjective and image-free contemplation.

An indication of the new consciousness is the fact that

many people can no longer believe in a God who can be conceived visually, and yet the "third eye of the mystic" (in Hugh of Saint-Victor's visual formulation) plays a decisive role in modern science.

> *The fairest thing we can experience is the mysterious. It is the fundamental emotion which stands at the cradle of true art and true science. A knowledge of the existence of something we cannot penetrate, of the manifestations of the profoundest reasons and the most radiant beauty, which are only accessible to our reason in their most elementary forms—it is this knowledge and this emotion that constitute the truly religious attitude; in this sense, and in this alone, I am a deeply religious man. [Albert Einstein,* The World As I See It, *trans. Alan Harris, New York, 1949, p. 5]*

28

An Answer to the New Longing
for Meditation

Never has the longing for meditation been so great in the West
as now. Needless to say, the word "meditation" is not always
meant in the way that the Christian tradition has understood
it. The reasons for this longing are largely psychological. We
seek sanctuary, threatened as we are with becoming victims
of the frantic pace of our technologized lives. Or, in the event
we have already become victims, we seek a means to become
spiritually healthy once again.

Yet there are also religious reasons for this longing. As soon
as we consider the religiosity of modern man, we become
aware of two things that at first glance seem to contradict each
other. Even as traditional faith continues to diminish, there
appears on a deeper level a great longing for God, often among
people of Christian upbringing who have nevertheless lost any
inner contact with the Church. Quite often these people do
not even know what their innermost search ultimately concerns. What they are offered in Christian worship, sermons,
and readings from Scripture no longer speaks to them. At
times it all seems to be merely superficial pretense, sometimes
even hypocrisy. These people feel themselves much more
drawn to non-Christian religions, especially to the meditation
practices employed in these religions. But there are also people
who, although they have not made a break with traditional
faith or the Church, nevertheless feel uncertain or very dissat-
isfied with the religious establishment. They see the whole
structure tottering; they see how so much once considered to
be indubitable has come into serious question or has even

been rejected outright. Questioning of this sort is no longer limited to people of another faith or no faith, as was the case somewhat earlier; it also occurs among those who should be leaders in their own ranks. There is much talk now of new interpretations of Scripture and of mysteries of faith like the Incarnation, the Resurrection of Christ and his Second Coming at the end of time. Even the fundamental mystery of God in Three Persons has come into question. In short, everything seems to have been shaken at its foundations. The paradox, then, is that reflection on these questions has only served to strengthen doubts rather than bring the certainty and peace we long for. Nevertheless, these people want to maintain their Christian faith and religious life at all costs and especially to deepen their experience of prayer. Thus many experience a great longing for meditation without always being able to account for what is going on inside.

There is no doubt that only a personal experience of faith or, more precisely, a personal experience of God can bring these people to their goal. The experience of God may be the most fundamental religious desire of modern man. Now, it is of course true that an experience of this sort, that which has been fittingly called "an encounter with God," is possible at any moment. It can break in upon us suddenly and without warning, a fact that many can give witness to. But such experiences are exceptions, and if we are seriously concerned with maintaining and deepening our faith we cannot expect the same thing to happen to us. We must make the effort ourselves, to the extent that this is possible; it should never be left to chance whether this light is to shine upon us or not. It would not, in any case, be a matter of chance but rather one of grace.

We are quite capable of such efforts, and the outlook for success is very promising along the way of meditation. The following is meant to give encouragement and provide helpful hints along this way. Here we shall speak very specifically about Christian meditation as a way to experience God. That is to say, we are not concerned with meditation as therapy, though meditation as a way of healing is also very important for modern people. We also do not concern ourselves here with controversies such as whether it is advisable for Christians to employ non-Christian meditation methods. Indeed, we shall not hesitate to learn as much as we can from other religions. As Saint Paul said, "Prove all things; hold fast that which is good." (1 Thess. 5:21). We also do not intend to prove that someone who has lost his Christian faith can find it again through practicing Eastern meditation, although there have been more than a few cases of this happening.

We direct our attention mainly to people who are psychologically healthy and who have maintained their Christian faith, to people who seek a way of meditation that is suitable for them both as Christians and as people of our time, with all their inhibitions, afflictions, and cares. It is also important to consider the time in which we live, since humanity is constantly evolving and in this moment has reached a decisive point in its development. That a person can and should also encounter God in other human beings, a point that is particularly stressed today, is not being questioned here. Nevertheless, we are concerned with a direct encounter with God, which does not occur in thoughts and words because it is nonrational.

29

Initial Difficulties

If we attempt to show the way to a form of meditation that leads to an experience of God, we immediately encounter an unexpected phenomenon: there are people who are, so to speak, born mystics. This does not mean they were born into the world as perfect human beings or saints. For this would only be possible when God himself became man or, to make use of conventional theological terminology, when there was a personal union between God and man. The fact is that many people, as soon as they reach the age of reason and religiously awaken to a degree, naturally pray and meditate in the style of mystics. They need only start to pray and everything turns inward and unites in a way that makes discursive thinking impossible. As far as method is concerned, they are already there where we wish to guide ordinary people not disposed in this way; they are already at a place which most people reach only after great struggle. For such mystically gifted individuals it would be a waste of time to attempt the development we are speaking of. Such persons would not be capable of doing so; the very attempt would be painful for them and a hindrance to their own religious striving—a fact proven by the experience of those who have nevertheless attempted it due to lack of proper guidance. Thus, we direct our attention not to these extraordinarily gifted individuals but rather to more ordinary people who take their religious life seriously and who wish to become complete persons. We address our remarks to people who strive for Christian perfection and who also wish to make use of meditation for this goal. Nevertheless, meditation alone is not enough to become perfect. Let us make one matter clear once and for all: if a person does not strive constantly to live a life free of sin and to overcome his baser instincts, no method of meditation can bring him any further along the spiritual path. He may seem to be successful, but eventually his own personal experience will bring him to the insight that he is on the wrong way—if he does not encounter even more calamitous things, like the man who built his house on sand: "And the rain descended, and the floods came, and the winds blew, and beat upon that house; and it fell: and great was the fall of it" (Matt. 7:27).

Here we limit our discussion to meditation. To be sure, we shall ascertain that meditation can be a unique means toward moral perfection. It can be mentioned in passing that a person with a propensity toward prayer received, as it were, as a gift in the cradle, should nonetheless always be aware of the need to prove himself worthy of this gift by striving toward moral perfection. Should he neglect this, he too could end up like the man who built this house on sand. Here lies a particular danger for the spiritually gifted. First of all, such people are usually not aware that they are gifted in this special way. They assume that everyone is the same until their first chance conversation with others about prayer, when they realize that they are the recipients of a special grace. Or they may read the writings of the mystics and find their own way of prayer described therein as such a special grace. After this, they avoid for the most part speaking about their particular ability, preferring to keep it a secret. They may try to seek out someone who can lead them along their spiritual path, but who can guide them? Here they often encounter great distress, feeling themselves to be misunderstood and thinking that people want to lead them from their own way, which was given to them without their having any choice about it.

Most people do not have any particular predisposition toward prayer. Should they nonetheless attempt to pray in this special way, having heard, perhaps, that this is a more perfect form of prayer, they soon encounter difficulties and will perhaps become discouraged to the point where they give up any further attempts.

30

Beginning the Practice of Meditation

In Christian circles it is customary to begin meditation with a method consciously and willfully concerned above all with reasoning and ideas. For example, we call to mind a passage or scene from the Gospels and mull over it. We may then imagine the situation, or ask what deeper meaning a phrase might have or why it was said and to whom. By so doing, we gain a deeper insight into the words and events being related, an insight that can be of great benefit in our moral and religious life. Such forms of meditation are especially familiar to Christians because for such people the Gospels are the true way of humanity; being Christian means living our lives according to the teachings and example of Christ. Nevertheless, this is not the only way that reason and will can operate in meditation. For example, we can imagine the presence of God in our own hearts and attempt to become ever more intimate with that presence. But here too, we are still actively involved with rational thinking; we do this consciously and willfully.

It can also happen that during our reading of the Gospels we encounter a word that has particular significance for us. It seems to speak to us in a special way, and we allow it to have its effect and sink into us. In the process, much that was vague before becomes clearer. Many things occur to us, sometimes regarding something that we should do, sometimes something that we should no longer do. In this way, decisions are made as if by themselves while at the same time we turn to God for enlightenment and strength. This type of meditation is still "objective" since it has an object which one concentrates on or toward which one consciously and willfully strives. Meditation of this sort is active and not passive; the individual ego leads the way.

The Christian tradition has a rich literature on the many forms of this meditation. Since not every Christian has a wide knowledge of the Scriptures, explanations and encouragement are provided to simplify such meditation on Biblical texts. In these forms of meditation, sufficient preparation is very important. In order to put ourselves in the right mood, so to speak, for the meditation, we should read the text attentively and consider on the previous evening what we are going to meditate on the next morning. Then it will be easier the following day to keep away the disturbing thoughts and concerns that would otherwise assault our consciousness and distract us during meditation.

It is undoubtedly beneficial and heartily recommended to everyone who wants to be a Christian in the fullest sense to employ this form of meditation, when possible every day. Anyone who does so will experience its blessed effects. This is easily observed and has been confirmed over centuries of religious practice. Until recently, at least, Westerners were advised to practice this form of meditation first. We could say that this form of meditation, for which Saint Ignatius of Loyola gives detailed instructions in his *Spiritual Exercises*, has been dominant in the West until today. This is true not only among Jesuits but also far beyond the bounds of that order in Christian and even non-Christian countries to the extent that Christians live there. Unfortunately, it has often been the case that people remain on the surface with this so-called "Ignatian method," and precisely for this reason it is often rejected now that we stand on the threshold of a new age. Ignatius was a mystic, and the superficial approach with which many have responded to his admittedly brief directions stands in crass contrast to the mystical depths that lie hidden in his Spiritual Exercises.

Whoever practices this or some other form of objective meditation will encounter new insights and deep solace. He or she will experience a growth of faith, hope, and love. But this is not always so. There will also be times when the meditator is distracted by thoughts throughout almost the entire period of meditation. He or she may experience a great dryness; time will go so slowly that the practitioner is tempted to break off before the allotted period has elapsed. Even Teresa of Ávila experienced this over a period of many years. Indeed, it is said that she seized the hourglass that stood beside her and shook it forcefully to make the time go faster!

Nevertheless, for a time meditation of this sort should bring a steady enrichment to people who are receptive to it or feel themselves drawn to it and practice regularly. However, there are probably only a special few for whom this will always be the case. After some time, most people will notice how the encouragement they experienced up to then through medita-tion decreases and finally disappears altogether in spite of their earnest efforts. It often happens that, as the result of a very active daily life, a certain weariness accumulates which then makes itself felt in the quietness of meditation. In spite of ourselves we end up asking, "Is there any sense in wasting precious time that could perhaps be better used in the service of my brothers and sisters?" To succumb to such temptations is surely not the answer. Nor would it be right to conclude that our way has been mistaken from the start. For meditation that is practiced consciously and willfully with the intellect, the will, and the imagination can provide great spiritual nourishment for a long period of time. Many things will become clear to the individual and much encouragement will have been gained, things for which we can be eternally grate-ful.

Questions of meditation aside, delving deeper into the Scriptures, particularly the Gospels, is also both desirable and essential for being Christian in the fullest sense of the word. In the event that such reading does not take place by way of meditation, it should nevertheless be undertaken or continued by pursuing another way devoted to reading and study.

Nevertheless, reading and study of this sort should never take the place of meditation. We have to be honest with ourselves; where does the reading stop and the meditation begin? The immediate answer is that they intermingle with each other, so that a clear distinction between them is impossible. To be sure, it is possible to combine them in such a way that we meditate in the process of turning inward in our reading and ruminating for a while over that which we have read. If, in order to avoid the difficulties mentioned, we fill out our meditation period in the way described with reading, pauses, and rumination as well as praying to God when we feel inspired to do so, we practice something that is certainly good and useful. But there is also the danger that we will thereby block the way to a deeper meditation. The time may come when excessive reading is a hindrance to that which is good in ourselves. We will be able to understand this better in the course of our exposition.

Meditation cannot remain on the surface; it must go deeper. This holds not only for the object of meditation but also for the meditating subject. The object must be grasped in its essence, and the meditator must not only grasp the object with the intellect but also make it his own in the depths of his soul. But this is not possible by simply reflecting on the object, for the process will actually be hindered by too much reflection. There are actual stages of prayer that are just as valid for Christian meditation. . . . These stages are as follows: (1) Prayer that is performed only verbally; (2) prayer that is executed with the intellect and consciously performed from start to finish; (3) prayer that penetrates the heart and is grasped with the emotions (due to the influence of grace); (4) prayer that is performed with the heart, which is continuous and leads finally to the highest ecstasy.

These stages cannot be reversed since they are based on human nature. They are also found in the Jesus Prayer, which has been practiced in the Eastern Church for more than a thousand years. In these steps, the nature of prayer makes a progression from outer to inner and simultaneously from active to passive. While at the beginning we are almost exclusively active, at the end we are in an almost totally passive state.

31

From Objective to Nonobjective Meditation

We have already concluded that objective meditation must sooner or later develop into meditation in the true sense of the word, that is, nonobjective or intuitive meditation. This has always been known and emphasized in Christian spirituality whenever the topic of mysticism arose. Mysticism has too long been considered a closed paradise where signs like "No entry!" "Watch your step!" and "Enter at your own risk!" hung at the entrance. Much has changed, and more is about to change. Nevertheless, we are still far from agreeing about what mysticism actually is. In the Western consciousness, the word "mysticism" evokes images of a dark, shadowy world whose experiences can provide no reliable or generally valid knowledge. Nevertheless, in spite of everything working against it and even though only a few have been aware of it, the "mystical stream" has continued unbroken in the Catholic Church. Undoubtedly the contemplative orders played the major role in keeping it alive. More recently, we hear opinions that tend toward the opposite extreme. Some people would have us believe that we are all mystics, especially the Christians among us since they are "in a state of grace."

Karl Albrecht, a modern German investigator of mystical states of consciousness, attempted a model of mysticism that would be valid for all Christian forms of mysticism as well as non-Christian forms. We shall return later to this topic. Here we propose a model of mysticism that was already tacitly taken for granted by many people regarding the Christian mystics.

The way from objective meditation to nonobjective meditation, a way that has been taught in Christian spirituality as a guide to mysticism, can be described briefly as follows. After having devoted plentiful time to meditation on the life of Christ and the Gospels, we progressively replace intellectual activity with the activity of the will. More concretely, meditation increasingly assumes the form of a dialogue with God or a short verbal utterance directed toward him. The next step is that whereby the activity of the will is simplified in the sense that there are no longer many "acts" (in the specifically prayerful sense) arising one after another but rather a single act (affect) focused on God for an extended period. It is, so to speak, a gaze or emotion directed toward God. When meditation has reached this stage, it is already meditation in the true sense. The consciousness is unified. . . . Then it is no longer very far to prayer involving concentration and stillness, states that are known as the first stages of mysticism.

Our attitude in prayer of this sort is no longer objective in the sense of thinking about something, as was the case earlier. Should we nevertheless attempt to do so, our unified state of consciousness would disappear. Such objective forms of prayer are also known as imperfect contemplation. Spiritual masters have always looked for a sign to occur during prayer of concentration that an individual is "called to" actual contemplation or, more precisely (since today we are more likely to say that everyone has this calling due to God's grace), can be expected to achieve it. In such cases, they have advised people to give up objective meditation altogether and instead turn inward and maintain an attitude of stillness. Such an attitude is very similar to the state encountered in the form of zazen known as *shikantaza*. The spiritual eye is simply turned inward. This is the Christian way to simple and deep prayer.

The transition from objective to nonobjective meditation can be problematic. Confining the intellect within certain bounds will occur naturally after a period of time. However, attempts to dwell for a long time in such a condition are often self-defeating; such states are not accessible through an act of will. This becomes self-evident if we recall that the soul is an organ in which spiritual feelings are born and not made. One might say that this can occur only as a result of a grace given by God. But is that really all that can be said in reply?

Many people pratice objective meditation for a while, in some cases with considerable success. But after a while their practice "dries up," so to speak. It doesn't work any more. Attempts to practice a purely "affective" form of meditation might be successful for a while, but usually they too turn out to be unsuccessful. If we then try to make things happen by an act of will, we may have temporary results until the day when this willful effort is seen as unnatural and we waver in our decision. For that which is being forced should actually happen by itself. Expressed in spatial terms, there is a spiritual "area" or state of consciousness wherein this happens by itself or where, at least, the possibility exists. If we succeed in arriving here, our situation becomes totally different. Such feelings are then given to us, they come from inside. And even if they do not come—which is also possible—the alternative is not a series of distractions or boredom or just spinning one's wheels. Anyone who has experienced the state of samadhi knows this is true. Time passes more quickly than when meditating with the intellect. The inner attitude is one of "gazing into the darkness," which is by no means same thing as simple contemplation of darkness. Saint John of the Cross calls such an attitude "dark contemplation." Speaking about this, he says that there is a light in the darkness that the soul cannot perceive because it is not purified enough. Others have referred to this darkness as "nothingness" (a term that is also used in Zen) and say that this is not darkness but rather a light of such intensity that the soul would be blinded by a direct gaze into its brightness.

32

Cistern Water and Spring Water: Two Ways to Experience God

In both ways it is God who is there at the end. This is an essential aspect of Christian meditation. With the first form, however, He is there as an object while with the second He is united with the subject. In the highest degree of experience there is no longer any awareness of a difference between God and the human spirit; this is the case in ecstatic union. What has been said concerning the first form is, incidentally, also true about the liturgy and private verbal prayer.

Putting all this together, we can say that the first form of experience takes place more or less on the surface of the spirit while the second takes place in the core of the soul. In prayer of concentration and silence, both the senses and one's psychic energy are brought back to the source; they are no longer acting independent of each another. Instead, a spring opens that flows from inside, directly from God, who dwells in the core of the soul. Johannes Tauler often expressed this idea in his writings. The first form resembles a cistern in which the water is from outside, either as rain or brought with human help. The second resembles the source water, which springs directly from the mountain. The water in the cistern is still and thus will become stagnant over time; the spring water is perpetually fresh. Moreover, anyone who tastes the spring water no longer has any desire to drink water from the cistern; it no longer tastes good. Tauler rebukes the "spiritual people," saying that as long as they are in a spiritual calling they draw their spiritual water from the cisterns and not from the core of the soul whence the pure source flows. As a result, these spiritual people are never purified of their failings such as envy and lack of love, despite the oral prayers to which they devote so many hours of their day. These people, says Tauler, allow themselves no time to go into their own spiritual depths.

This comparison of the two forms of meditation already shows us that the first form, which we normally practice at the outset in accordance with our human nature, cannot be the final form if our goal is to be truly transformed by meditation. The Christian has admittedly come into grace through the merit of Christ and one's own freely-willed turning to God, and has in truth become a child of God, but a child who now must grow to adulthood in order to become a complete child of God: that is, another Christ. Meditation plays an extremely important role in this growth process. Nevertheless, it cannot fulfill its goal if it is still concerned with the objective world. For the person to be transformed fundamentally, objective meditation must sooner or later be replaced by nonobjective meditation, which takes place in the core of the soul. Speaking about this, Tauler talks about the "Kehre" or "turning" that must occur in the soul at some point if a person is to become truly perfect. Thus it is completely in keeping with things and is part of the overall healing process that the starting form of meditation should "dry up" after a while. We should not conclude from this that it would be better to give up meditation altogether and instead return to reading with meditative pauses. Rather, the time has come to change to another, deeper type of meditation, to that second form which is perfected in the core of the soul. And this is mystical prayer.

33

Mystical Experience, East and West

Mystics have always been convinced that mystical experience provides them with reliable knowledge. In particular, awareness of the presence of the unknowable (in Christian terms: God) came into their own hearts with irrefutable evidence. They already knew about this presence, due to their Christian faith. But it remained a dark understanding, the sort against which there is always the possibility of doubt even when there do not seem to be any reasonable grounds for doubt. In contrast, in mystical experience all doubt becomes impossible, just as we cannot doubt the presence of someone standing right in front of us. The same holds for certain experiences in other religions. Zen enlightenment, for example, is "without doubt a phenomenon involving true, pure, direct and experiential understanding of the all-embracing totality" (Karl Albrecht, *Das Mystische Erkennen*, Bremen, 1958, p.48). It is admittedly, as was said, a nonpersonal experience of the absolute, but this, as we shall see, strengthens conviction rather than weakens it, provided, of course, that the experience is genuine—a provision that also holds for experiences in the Christian sphere. . . .

Is the personal element in Christian mysticism based only on one of the established categories of thinking and understanding? It is true that a nonpersonal experience of the absolute will seldom occur to a Christian with faith in God. However, if it were totally impossible, a Christian could never experience genuine Zen enlightenment, for such an experience is definitely impersonal. The fact is that Christians have experienced Zen enlightenment and had their experiences confirmed by authentic Zen masters. In most instances, when a Christian experiences enlightenment during the practice of Zen meditation, he or she assumes this to be an experience of God. Nevertheless, the materials at our disposal are still too limited to allow any final conclusions on this matter. In the dialogue between Christian and Zen Buddhist mysticism, it is sometimes asked which of the two has the ultimate experience. The Buddhist believes that the Christian has not yet come to the final goal so long as God is still experienced as a person. In reply, the Christian says that the Buddhist must go a step further in order to come to the ultimate, which is the personal God.

34

The Third Eye of the Mystic and the Experience of Hugh of Saint-Victor

Religious truths cannot be completely understood in a rational manner. This holds for the teachings of Eastern religions as well as those of Christianity. Particularly in the last few decades, we have become more attentive in Christianity to this mysterious character of faith. Merely rational thinking allows no inner access to undivided existence, which is known in the Christian cultural sphere as "God," but which can also be termed the Absolute, the nameless, or whatever. As long as we only grasp this conceptually, it is not God but rather merely a picture of God. Precisely this has become apparent to the many people in the West today who are no longer able to believe in a "conceptualized" God or to imagine God as an object. The fact that a God capable of being an object of contemplation is already dead for many people is itself an indication of a new consciousness. Many of the Christian mystics have gone through the painful experience of nonobjectification of God. Only through "the dark night of the soul," to repeat the words of Saint John of the Cross, only through the renunciation of everything that can be imagined or objectified were they able to approach God. . . .

The "insight" in the sense of an effect resulting from Zen meditation belongs without doubt to the intuitive forms of knowledge. It is not exactly the same thing as the direct methods of knowing described above, means that every individual possesses to some extent and uses constantly without giving any thought to them. For example, we all know that the same thing cannot both be and not be at the same time.

In contrast, "insight" in the Zen sense is not possessed by everyone just because we are human, for not everyone is a mystic or becomes one at a certain age in the same way that we all eventually awaken to the use of reason. In referring to such insight, we could use the traditional metaphor of the "third eye" that we possess in addition to our physical eye and the eye of rational understanding. Speaking in this sense, the twelfth-century Christian mystic Hugh of Saint-Victor said that originally we had three eyes—the physical eye, the eye of understanding, and the third eye of contemplation, which last was totally blinded in Man's fall from grace.

PART FIVE

ZEN AND CHRISTIANITY

Enomiya-Lassalle began his Zen training in 1943 and has been conducting Zen courses regularly in Europe since the East-West Conference held at Elmau, West Germany, in 1967.

Zen is a way of meditation that traces its roots back to ancient India. Lassalle himself is a disciple of the renowned Japanese Zen master Harada Sogaku Roshi, who combined the two classical Zen schools of Soto and Rinzai to form a new school that is now being continued by Lassalle and others. Father Lassalle continues to emphasize the inner attitude in practice, for without that access to the deepest layers of consciousness is not possible.

In the meantime, other Westerners have followed Lassalle's example and have become Zen masters. The training and testing that a candidate undergoes is extremely arduous; the difficult process of solving several hundred koans is only the first step. Only a select few have actually been given permission to teach as Zen masters. For disciples the Zen master is not just any teacher but the Buddha himself.

Enomiya-Lassalle initially had difficulties with the Vatican authorities following the release of his first book, Zen-Weg zur Erleuchtung *(1958; 6th ed., 1981). The book was finally taken off the Index during the Second Vatican Council, an event that opened a window on the East. Since then, Enomiya-Lassalle has continued on his own way with unshakable conviction. He has already led many of his students to the actual goal, the experience of enlightenment, something that was once believed to be possible only for the spiritually gifted but is now becoming a reality for many. This experience of the Absolute leads to a perfect unity wherein life and death are no longer seen as separate from each other.*

> *A monk once asked the great Chinese Zen master Zhaozhou of the Tang Period [Japanese, Joshu, 778–897], "What is enlightenment?"*
> *Zhaozhou said, "I can't hear you."*
> *The monk repeated his question.*
> *Zhaozhou said, "I am not deaf, you know."*
> *Then Zhaozhou composed a poem:*

He who moves freely on the great Way,
Reaches the gate of enlightenment.
"Just sit," and the Mind is boundless.
Every year is spring, once again spring.

35

What Is Zen?

The word "Zen" originates from the Sanskrit word *dhyana*, which means "meditation." The Chinese wrote this word with a single character pronounced *ch'an,* a word that had previously been used in Taoist circles. The character is a combination of the ideograms for "God" and for "one" or "simple"; together they mean "one with God." As time went on, the word "Zen" gradually took on a broader meaning to eventually include everything having any connection with this form of meditation. For example, included now in the larger field of Zen are the well-known tea ceremony, or *chado,* and the art of archery, or *kyudo.* The same holds true for kendo (swordsmanship), judo, karate, calligraphy, and flower arrangement. From the Zen standpoint, none of these are merely sports or hobbies, but they are "ways" in the deepest sense of the word. They breathe the breath of Zen; that is to say, they contain the spiritual approach to life which Zen embodies. All of these Zen ways are known to a greater or lesser extent in the West today and are practiced by a growing number of people. All of them have their individual methods and meanings as well as their particular effects on the practitioner. To attempt to describe them all would be straying too far from our topic. Nevertheless, we can mention here that the most basic and the most effective of these ways remains Zen meditation, or zazen.

36

The Origin of Zazen

As early as the sixth century B.C. the Buddha himself had adopted the lotus posture, the classic Asian meditation position, from yoga. But it was the Indian Buddhist monk Bodhidharma who is traditionally considered to have been the actual founder of zazen. In 526 A.D., about a thousand years after the Buddha, Bodhidharma came from India to southern China and started the school of meditation from which Zen developed. Bodhidharma taught the type of meditation that was common to his own Buddhist tradition, that of the so-called Mahayana school. (Other Buddhist countries, such as Sri Lanka, Burma, and Thailand, were characterized by differing practices, which is why the spread of zazen was not identical with the spread of Buddhism.)

Bodhidharma's teachings on meditation later incorporated many elements from various philosophical and meditative schools already present in China, particularly Taoism, with which Zen came into close contact at that time.

It would be straying too far from our topic, and it is not necessary for our purposes, to trace these developments in detail. After its fusion with Chinese spiritual life was completed, there were no significant changes in Zen. The Zen tradition came to Japan via Korea between the seventh and twelfth centuries. But even after Zen had been introduced into Japan, for centuries Zen students continued to travel to the great Chinese masters for instruction. Even the koans, a certain form of conundrum given to Zen students that we shall discuss later, trace their origin almost exclusively back to the old Chinese masters. This means that most of them are almost a thousand years old.

Brief as it is, this outline of Zen's historical development is enough to explain why, even today, there are various approaches to Zen and different interpretations of it. There are two main schools, Soto and Rinzai. They both developed to their present form in the twelfth century, the zenith of Zen in Japan, and can be distinguished from each other even today by their differing characters. We shall attempt to delineate the most important differences in interpretation and practice between these two later in this study.

37

The Practice of Zen Meditation

Zazen means "sitting meditation," which already hints at the important role that sitting plays in this practice. The practice is concerned with three things in particular: bodily posture, breathing and inner attitude.

Bodily posture: One sits on a cushion about 6 centimeters thick, which is placed either directly on the floor or on a blanket. The right foot is then placed on the left thigh and the left foot on the right thigh (see Fig.1, opposite). This sitting posture, known as the full lotus posture, is undoubtedly the best, although when necessary it can be modified to the half lotus by placing only one foot on the opposite thigh and leaving the other foot on the ground under the opposite thigh (see Fig. 2). Other possible modifications include sitting on the heels (see Fig. 3). If you are incapable of sitting on the floor in any of these positions, it is possible to sit on a chair, though you should be careful not to lean forward and also to keep the spine straight and the head erect (see Fig. 4).

The upper torso should be perfectly straight, as should the head, but also completely relaxed. Your arms should be relaxed and hang down naturally at your sides. Your hands should be placed on top of each other with the palms facing up and the thumbs lightly touching. Your eyes should be half open and, although the eyes should not focus on anything, your angle of vision should fall naturally on a point about a meter away.

Breathing: As a rule, breathing should be diaphragmatic, and one breathes through the nose. There should be no

excessive pauses between inhalations and exhalations, nor should you hold your breath. Although we shall speak soon about the deeper significance of this technique, we can mention here that the positions and breathing just described stimulate circulation and calm the nerves. Once the body has come to rest in this way, it is easier to achieve the state of peace so necessary for meditation.

Inner attitude: This is the most important point of all, since it is the direct aim of the physical posture and breathing. Nevertheless, by its very nature, it is more difficult to describe than the other two.

Dogen Zenji (1200–1252), Japanese Zen master and founder of the Soto school, advised his students to "think not-thinking." In other words, we are concerned with a state of nonthinking, which nevertheless is not the same thing as dozing on one's cushions. Another way to describe this inner attitude is: "without concepts and without thoughts (*munen musō*). Zazen thus could be described as meditation without an object or theme. When beginning meditation in the Christian tradition, we are accustomed, at least in the initial stages, to concentrating on an object, whether it be an article of faith or a scriptural passage. In Zen, things are different: there is no reflection, not even on Buddhist teachings. The ancient Chinese Zen master Lin-chi (Japanese, Rinzai) said:

> Remove every hindrance from the way. . . . If you meet the Buddha on the Way, kill the Buddha. If you meet your ancestors, kill your ancestors. If you meet your father and mother, kill your father and mother. If you meet disciples of the Buddha, kill them. If you meet your relatives, kill your relatives. Only in this way will you reach salvation, only in this way will you escape the entangling nets and become free.

What Rinzai means, of course, is that you should dispense with thoughts of the Buddha, disciples, relatives and the like whenever they occur to you during zazen.

That this condition of nonthinking is not a total absence of psychological activity is confirmed by recent experiments in which brain waves and galvanic skin response were monitored during zazen. When advanced students such as Zen monks practiced zazen, they produced alpha waves and later theta waves.

To summarize the inner attitude to be cultivated during zazen, we attempt to turn off all ego-directed activity. The ego should be passive, receptive, open. It is, to use a simile, not an attitude of speaking but rather one of hearing, although we do not of course actually attempt to concentrate on external sounds, since that would be just another ego-directed activity. We must delve into the deeper levels of consciousness while nevertheless not forcing anything; it must be allowed to happen.

Three methods of concentration can be used as aids to achieve this inner attitude: (1) Concentration on one's breathing; (2) Practice with a koan; (3) Just sitting, without recourse to such "crutches." Let us examine these three methods one by one.

Concentration on the breath can be done in a number of ways. It is common practice to begin by counting the breaths, usually from one to ten, after which one starts from one again. The inhalations are counted on the odd numbers and the exhalations on the even numbers. Another method consists not in counting the breaths but rather following them with the mind's eye, so to speak. Concentrating on the breath in these simple ways, regardless of the method of concentration, helps first of all to limit the formation of thoughts and then to sink into the deeper layers of consciousness. This method of concentrating on one's breaths is, incidentally, not unique to Zen. Like the lotus posture, it traces its origins back to pre-Buddhist times. Originally, it was not simply a technical aid; it had an even deeper meaning. Breath is life. Although we can survive long periods without food, we die after only a few minutes if we cannot breathe. Perhaps this is why earlier cultures were so convinced that the breath has a very close kinship with the spiritual. Indeed, the same word was often used for both.* In the biblical account of creation, for example, God breathes the breath of life into man's face after He has formed him from the earth. Of course, it would only be a distraction to reflect about the breath in this way during zazen. But perhaps knowing something about the interrelations of

*As we can see in the English word "spirit" and its cognates.—Trans.

these elements can help to make breath-counting somewhat more approachable for the beginner.

The second aid to practice is *concentration on a koan*. The koan (Chinese, *kung-an*) is a short text containing a puzzle or paradox for which there is no rational answer. Although it is customary for the master to give the student some preliminary explanation of the koan, even such explanations are not immediately understandable if one has not already gained some insight into Zen. There are about 1,700 koans in Zen, most of them in the form of "mondo," an exchange of "question" *(mon)* and "answer" *(do)* between master and student. Here are some examples.

A monk asked Master Joshu if even a dog has Buddha-nature. Joshu said, "Wu" (Japanese, *mu,* literally "no" or "no thing").

Once a monk asked Joshu, "Master, I am a newcomer here. Show me the Way." Joshu said, "Have you finished your breakfast?" The monk said, "I have." Joshu said, "Then go and wash out the bowls." The monk came to realization.

The Japanese master Hakuin clapped his hands, then held up a hand and asked his students, "Can you hear the sound of one hand?"

Many Zen students have reached enlightenment with the aid of a koan. We can imagine this process to occur in approximately the following manner: The student first attempts to find a logical solution to the koan. It eventually becomes clear to him that no solution can be found in this way. This puts an end to logical thinking. In the meantime, however, he has become so caught up in the problem that he can no longer free himself of it. And all the while he continues to be summoned time after time to his master and challenged to give an answer. He is—to use a well-known Zen simile—

like someone who has swallowed a red-hot ball and must spit it out, but is unable to do so.

This is the state of "great doubt" often mentioned in Zen. Wherever the student goes, the koan follows him. It is in his mind constantly; he is, one might say, preoccupied with it day and night. Then comes the time when he feels that he himself has become the problem: He himself has become the "no thing" that Joshu spoke of; his individual self has disappeared and he has become Hakuin's single hand. If he perseveres in his practice, the koan itself disappears from his consciousness. Now there is only the total emptiness of the consciousness, which is a prerequisite for enlightenment. At this point in most cases only the most ordinary sense perception is needed—it could be the sound of a temple bell or the barely perceptible sound of a leaf falling from a tree—for the spirit to open. The great experience has happened.

Although koans have certainly been very effective, they remain a means; koans in themselves are not the essence of Zen. Thus, the use of koans varies according to the Zen school and according to the particular master. Of the two major sects of Soto and Rinzai, the former as a rule does not use koans while the latter uses them frequently. In fact, students in the Rinzai school wishing to become Zen masters must solve all the koans, a process that alone requires many years.

The third way to enlightenment is "shikantaza" or "just-sitting," as it can be literally translated. It receives this name because one sits and breathes in the way described already, but without employing any aid, neither concentrating on one's breaths nor practicing with a koan. When thoughts come, one neither follows them nor tries to drive them away. A master of more recent times, Harada Sogaku Roshi, once described it as follows:

> You are like Mount Fuji towering majestically over the ocean. The green mountains surrounding you stand immovable. The white clouds come and go. . . . But

even this comparison is lacking in force. It would be better to say that your zazen is something so massive that it feels as if the sitting cushion is the earth itself and the universe fills your lower torso. Think not-thinking. This is the key to zazen, this is zazen's mainspring.

38

The Master

We come now to a very important topic, the personal guidance of the student by a Zen master. From the Zen point of view, the main reason for this guidance is that true Zen, especially enlightenment, can only be transmitted by initiation into its mysteries and not by theoretical instructions.

Zen is more than just a technique or method. It contains something spiritual that should be transmited from master to disciple: that is, an experience of the greatest profundity. For this reason, guidance by the Zen master has always been considered to be an essential element in Zen practice. The deep significance of this can be expressed most clearly with a ceremony. For the student the Zen master is not just another teacher but the Buddha himself. Thus, the student approaches the Zen master on his knees, making three to nine full prostrations and then, still on his knees, approaches to within twenty centimeters of the master. During these personal interviews, which take place in a special room reserved for that purpose, the student is allowed to talk only about matters directly pertaining to practice. He may speak about a particular experience or some difficulty encountered in practice, often expressing this in the form of questions directed to the master. Sometimes such interviews last less than a minute, since this is usually enough for the master to perceive how the student is doing in his practice. The master has a small handbell next to his seat which he rings to end the interview. The student leaves immediately and returns to the Zen hall to continue meditation.

Anyone who aspires to Zen practice is free to choose the

master he or she wants. Once the choice has been made, however, and the individual has been accepted as a student by a particular master, it is customary to refrain from changing masters. Leading Zen masters often make applicants wait for a long time, even putting them off with harsh words, to see whether their intentions are serious. Nevertheless, if someone should need to change his master, another rule now takes precedence. He must forget all the teachings he has received from his former master and allow himself to be guided by his new master, free of preconceptions.

39

Goals and Effects

It is now the proper place in our study to ask two important questions: (1) What is the actual goal of this meditation? (2) What significance does it have for the person as such—that is, regardless of whether he or she is a Buddhist or a Christian, an Oriental or a Westerner?

The goal of zazen is very clearly determined by its Buddhistic origins. It is awakening to our "Buddha-nature" which, according to Buddhist teaching, each of us is intrinsically endowed with. Thus, we are not being asked to become something that we have not been, but rather to become aware of what we have been from the start.

By its very essence, this concept of Buddha-nature is not something that concerns Buddhists alone. We are concerned with an overall conception of what we could call the "double being" which each person has or is. One being is that part of our existence that we are all aware of. But that is not all. Each person also participates in an undivided absolute being, which is the basis of all that is. According to Buddhist teaching, however, we should do more than participate in this absolute being: we must also become aware of it. In the moment when this happens one experiences how what one assumed to be "I" is actually not one's self from a greater perspective. In this experience, we become aware of another, supra-wordly, supra-individual existence. This is the heart of the experience that we attempt to describe with the much-used term *enlightenment*.

Nevertheless, with such an experience Zen meditation has not yet fulfilled its goal, and the practice must be continued.

This experience of enlightenment is only an initial glimmer, a small light in the depths of the soul that must become brighter and brighter until it encompasses everything and all thoughts, words, and actions emerge directly from it.

Then occurs that state of which Saint Paul wrote: "It is no longer I who live, but Christ who lives in me" (Gal. 2:20). This quotation is known to many Zen masters, who use it sometimes with their Western students to clarify the final goal of zazen. We shall speak more of this later.

In answering the second question about what significance Zen meditation has for the individual, we cannot limit ourselves to the final goal of enlightenment. Even on the way to enlightenment much occurs that is of great value not only for Buddhists but for everyone. It is to these effects of Zen meditation that we now turn. The effects can be grouped into two main categories: (a) certain powers which we acquire through the practice of Zen; (b) insight, or intuitive powers of knowledge.

The first powers mentioned are of a physico-somatic and psychic-spiritual sort. We limit ourselves here to the spiritual powers that are awakened or liberated through zazen. These primarily involve the ability to check the usual scattered state of mind and thereby create spiritual balance and inner peace.

Let us consider briefly what this means in concrete terms. First of all, we become masters of our own emotions and thus gain peace of mind and inner freedom. We control our feelings instead of the other way around. Nevertheless, this does not imply passive indifference or a loss of energy or emotionality. Today as in the past, people from all walks of life have practiced zazen, among them statesmen and magnates of industry. The ability to collect our scattered spirits is experienced as an increased ability to concentrate, which as we know is crucial in any activity. Thus, we are able to concentrate even when outer and inner hindrances interfere.

The type of balance that is necessary between emotionality and peace of mind is well explained by Johannes Heinrich

Schultz, the founder of autogenic training. Schultz says that we must be careful that the stimuli to which we are daily subjected do not take hold in the vegetative. When this is prevented, they are naturally absorbed and experienced, though they dissipate more quickly. However, if they go deep into the body, they establish themselves there like a hook that cannot be pulled out again. Then the same "film sequence," so to speak, continues to run over and over.

There is another way to explain the effect of zazen. In Zen we often speak about the front and the back of the mind or heart,* aspects that are differentiated in somewhat the same way as conscious and unconscious activity. The activity at the front is known to us, we have it more or less in our grasp; but many people do not know at all what is happening at the back of the mind. They think that they are free and objective in their decisions when actually they are led by their unconscious to a far greater extent than they suppose. In zazen, one comes to know the back of one's own mind. Perhaps the best comparison is psychological self-analysis. "One suddenly understands the true state of the heart" is how one person described his own enlightenment.

Naturally, all this has an effect on the religious aspect of our lives too. Increased ability to concentrate means it becomes easier to keep attentive when praying and attending liturgical ceremonies. Increased self-control and inner freedom make it easier to be of service to others. And this no doubt leads to a form of ethical perfection. Whatever is negative and aberrant is gradually eliminated; it is "meditated away," so to speak. Envy, hatred, and dissatisfaction disappear or lose the objects to which they were directed; the individual becomes freer and capable of true love.

The second effect of zazen is insight. Human knowledge takes two forms: discursive and intuitive, although countless combinations lie in between these two poles. Discursive knowing proceeds logically from one truth to another. Intuitive

*The Japanese word *kokoro* means both "mind" and "heart."—Trans.

knowing recognizes the truth directly. The former, by its very nature, is directed to individual things, the second primarily to the one absolute existence. There is a close connection between these two ways of knowing—a connection that can be only hinted at, although much attests to how discursive thinking is superseded by intuitive thinking.

Thomas Merton, who spent the latter part of his life as a monk in a Trappist monastery and also found his way to the wisdom of the Far East, is considered one of the foremost mystics of this century. He once formulated the relationship between the discursive and intuitive in the following way:

> Every philosophy and theology which is clear about the meaning of the true order of things seeks to go through the clouds to the top of the mountain where we hope to meet the living God. Every science must be filled with the consciousness of its limits and the longing for a living experience of truth which is not reachable with speculative thinking.*

What we are experiencing today in the sciences seems to confirm this view. For precisely the most distinguished scientists are now seeking the way through diversity to unity and thus to ultimate existence, to that no longer comprehensible with discursive thinking. Applying this to Christian meditation, we see that any meditation that is objectively concerned with details can give us only inadequate insight into religious truths. This is especially true for knowledge of the Absolute in the Christian sense of a personal God. For this Absolute, this God, is beyond all categories, concepts, and verbal expression. Many people have lost their faith because they could find no way to penetrate deeper into the mystery of God beyond conventional discursive thinking. Today many people find it impossible to accept an anthropomorphic conception of God, no matter how much they try. As long as we attempt to

*This passage has been translated from the German, as the author did not cite the source of the original English quotation from Merton.—Trans.

grasp God with concepts we actually do not grasp God Himself but only a picture of Him.

It is for this reason that meditation cannot remain concerned with specifics; it must become intuitive, nondiscursive meditation.

In our time we are experiencing the very important encounter between Christianity and Buddhism, particularly the forms of Buddhism represented in Zen. The insight or the capacity for intuitive perception that is encouraged in Zen practice is exactly the same ability that more often than not has been lost to the Christians of our time.

Even today, people in the East recognize an "organ" for intuitive understanding. It is the "ground" or the "core of the soul," the "third eye" of mystics. We in the West are accustomed to reducing spiritual feelings to understanding and reason. For example, when we recognize something or some person as good and worthy of love, our will then creates an act of love directed toward that object. But people in the East say that such love must not be willed but rather "conceived and born" in the "ground" or "core" of the soul. This core is like a "spiritual soil" from which all feelings and perceptions spring forth. Religious feelings too, especially faith, can only arise in this way. Mere effort of will is not enough, even if we have the best knowledge at our disposal. In Western culture, this spiritual soil has been overgrown or become sterile through overemphasis on the materialistic and the rationalistic. This has resulted in the spiritual crisis of our time, whose signs we encounter everywhere. Zen meditation addresses this ground; it makes it fruitful again precisely because it disregards discursive thinking.

That brings us to the question of how all this should actually take place. We must always remember that zazen is a way of contemplation and thus, like all true ways of contemplation, a way of purification. For example, it is a prerequisite for those wishing to travel the way of enlightenment that they be prepared to observe the Buddhist commandments and lead morally pure lives. Thus daily life in Zen monasteries is very strict in many respects. For instance, there are seven-day training courses during which participants are not allowed to sleep at all.

Probably no other religion contains so radical an approach to this process of spiritual "stripping-away." Anyone who embarks upon this path under the direction of a strict Zen master will notice this soon enough. We cannot cling to anything, we can never stay where we are on the path, regardless of whether our own thoughts and feelings are good or bad. The slightest exception would mean a halt on the way. Anyone who has set out on his way in earnest cannot go back again, can never be the same as before. For the individual experiences things which are unforgettable. We cannot help it, we must go deeper and deeper into the darkness until the light we long for finally reveals itself. As to when this happy moment occurs, no one knows. Indeed, we never have any guarantee that we will ever come to the light. We know only one thing, that our time has not been wasted if we persevere. We will notice how our life is being transformed, and realize that we are capable of more—not least in the service of our fellow human beings—than would have been possible had we not set out on this path.

40

Enlightenment

Enlightenment is the actual goal of Zen, but no conceptual explanation of enlightenment is really possible. Although now we shall nevertheless attempt such an explanation, it is primarily to stress that enlightenment is not a matter of gaining knowledge of something new. In other words, we do not know any more than we did before. Nevertheless, we know what we have always known in a new way. Beyond any doubt it is experiential knowing and not theoretical knowing that is attained in enlightenment. And yet the dimensions of this experience can be immense. When Kosen Imakita, a Japanese Zen monk of the Meiji period, attained enlightenment, he cried out, "A million sutras [Buddhist scriptures] are nothing but a candle to the sun."

What is actually experienced in enlightenment? We can give as least two answers. First of all, we experience something that could be called the true self, the deeper self, as opposed to the empirical self. It is the immediate experience of one's own existence, a "direct perception of self," which differs both quantitatively and qualitatively from everyday consciousness, and which is therefore almost impossible to describe in words.

The same holds for the second answer to the question about the content of enlightenment: the experience of undivided, absolute reality. This reality can be experienced either as personal or as impersonal.

Hardly anyone today would question whether Zen enlightenment and similar experiences in other non-Christian religions are genuine experiences of the Absolute, even though they are impersonal in nature. Were they personal in nature, they would be the same as an experience of God in the Christian sense. The formulation of this experience, and in particular the attempt to contain it in concepts, will take different forms according to one's prevailing view of the universe. Genuine mystical experience resists all attempts at conceptual expression. This means that anyone who attempts to do so will utilize the categories available, although this, by its very nature, can easily lead to misunderstandings.

In enlightenment, the Buddhist experiences his deepest self as one with absolute existence and is strengthened as a result in his faith in the nonduality of all existence. The Christian, and anyone else who believes in a personal God, experiences the self not only in himself but also in his relation to an absolute personal reality. He experiences God in himself. That is to say, the self does not "melt into" the Absolute. Nevertheless, as Meister Eckhart says, "Thus is God my ground and my ground is God's ground." This refers to the loving union with God that is so typical of Christian mysticism. Both practitioners, the Buddhist and the Christian, experience freedom from fear and doubt as well as deep peace and joy. Whether interpreted in a Buddhist or a Christian sense, enlightenment is undoubtedly a precious experience—indeed, rightly understood, perhaps the most precious experience man is capable of. When we hear or read of the enlightenment experiences of the great masters and study them in some detail, the wish arises to experience this world for ourselves— but we do not usually dare to hope that this will ever become a reality for us too.

Nevertheless, it is not impossible for us too to attain at least a small enlightenment—although the right conditions need to be created for this, especially total dedication and correct guidance. Indeed, recently cases of Westerners too coming to enlightenment through Zen practice are no longer so rare.

Something which should make us even more hopeful, however, is an increasingly pronounced development of the person in this direction of a unified experience of the world. Enlightenment is certainly an essential aspect of this new dimension. And this is true for the Zen experience as well as for Christian mysticism.

On both spiritual paths, in the last few years such experiences have become so numerous that we can say with authority that what was previously accessible only to a few blessed individuals can now become reality for many. The person of the future can and will be a mystic if he or she makes use of the opportunity which is given.

41

Kosen Imakita:
"Like One Risen from the Dead"

This effect of zazen, that is, enlightenment or "seeing the essence," is beyond all concepts. It cannot be grasped through any philosophy or worldview, for it is not bound to any of these. It is a pure fact that nevertheless has the power to free us from all anxiety and fear. Such feelings fall away from us like a dirty garment. The Japanese master Dogen Zenji, expressed the moment of his enlightenment with the words "Body and mind have fallen away."

Today there are already quite a number of personal enlightenment accounts, including some reported by Westerners. Here, however, I wish to introduce the story of the Japanese monk Kosen Imakita because I find it particularly instructive.

> One night as I was deep in meditation, I suddenly found myself in a very curious state. It was as if I were dead. Everything had been cut away. There was no longer any before and after. Self and object were gone. The only thing I felt was how the inside of my self was totally unified and filled with everything that was over, under and around me. . . . After a while I came back to myself like one risen from the dead. My seeing, hearing, speaking, my actions and my thoughts were completely different from what they had been up to then. As I hesitantly attempted to reflect on the truths of the world and to grasp the meaning of the ungraspable, I understood everything.

An experience of this sort cannot be expressed adequately in concepts. Everything conceptual already contains an interpretation within itself; it is no longer the matter itself. Keeping this in mind, we can nevertheless say that enlightenment is an experience of absolute reality. We avoid using the word "God," because it has connotations of particular cosmological ideas that would limit our conception of this experience—which contradicts the very nature of the experience itself. Anyone who has had this experience knows that there is this other world, regardless of whether or not one believed in it previously. Many people have experienced this essential oneness of existence, often independently of any Zen practice or any other form of meditation. Nevertheless, the experience of the essential oneness of all things is not the whole of Zen enlightenment; it is only one aspect.

Does a transformation of consciousness occur with this experience, not just in the moment of the experience itself, but also later so that something more remains than just a pleasant memory? For most people who have had such an experience without any conscious preparation for it, it survives as little more than a memory. They don't know what to do with the experience. If they tell someone about it, they are not understood; indeed, in some cases they might be sent to a psychiatrist. If such people eventually come to Zen, often many years later, they can tell the Zen master of their experience and thus come to the first real understanding of that experience—although the Zen master may not recognize their experience as enlightenment in the full sense. But even if he should confirm the experience as authentic, he will tell them that they must now meditate a great deal in order to integrate the experience into their lives. If his advice is followed, a lasting transformation of the religious consciousness will eventually take place.

To be sure, we must distinguish here between "great enlightenment" and "small enlightenment." Although the same supreme reality is experienced in both cases, there can be great differences in depth. Great enlightenment, an experience such as that encountered by the Buddha, brings with it a deep transformation of consciousness, as far as we can surmise from reports. The same holds true, for example, for Ramana Maharshi, an Indian whose experience occurred without any preparation at the age of sixteen—an experience so deep that it took years before he integrated it and could interact with others in a normal way. Thereafter he was able to help many people along their inner way, until he left this world about thirty years ago.

When, through continued practice, enlightenment is truly integrated, a new consciousness matures, so to speak, in which we no longer come to decisions as a result of reflecting and weighing the consequences but rather immediately and with complete certainty. Then a passage from Johannes Tauler shows itself to be true: "Then a person knows immediately what he should do, what he should ask for and what he should preach about."

PART SIX

THE TRANSPARENCY OF GOD IN EVERYDAY LIFE

When man is freed from the restrictions of space-time and has forged his way to a new consciousness of the fourth dimension, he will experience, in the process of prevailing over all dualism, the undivided whole that Teilhard called the Divine Milieu. As Enomiya-Lassalle continually stresses, the way of man goes beyond its present stage toward perfection. In ever-increasing degrees, the structures that are valid today become obsolete, and in the process we outgrow our need for dogmas.

The way to liberation and freedom from the ego leads us beyond objective meditation to transparency of the unconsciousness. Our lives will be a perception of the present, a continuous experience of the moment, which by its timelessness becomes eternity. Both the quest for the source and the way to the core of the soul will always be bound up with religious experience. The question whether the present form of the churches is a help or a hindrance in the discovery of divine reality can be left unanswered for the time being. What is of ultimate and exclusive validity is our goal, for which nonobjective meditation can be recommended as a valid way. In integral, cosmic consciousness, man will experience the totality-unity as timeless and unchanging.

Who will hold the heart of man so that it can stand still and then see how eternity, which always remains still, is neither past nor yet to come?   [Augustine]

42

The Divine Milieu

The transformation in thinking that we see in different areas of life shows that the new consciousness has already begun to make its presence felt. Rational thinking is no longer exclusively valid. We have broken through the confines that have restrained us for more than two millennia. The fourth dimension is already having an effect, even if it is not yet alive in our everyday consciousness. In many areas the philosophy of "either-or," of *non datur tertium* (the principle of contradiction) which until recently seemed so impossible to transcend, has already been done away with. If this had occurred in even a single area of thinking it would have been enough, since the essence of this principle is the idea that there are no exceptions. The whole of traditional philosophy is on the verge of toppling.

Perspectival thinking has also been largely transcended by a new dimension of human consciousness that defies rational understanding. And that is how it should be, since if the new consciousness could be comprehended rationally, it would show that we had not yet emerged from rational thinking. To be sure, such signs only indicate the possibility of realizing this new dimension and by no means indicate its total integration in human consciousness. This was also true for the process of integrating the consciousness structures that preceded it.

With this development, however, we finally become aware of the possibility of freeing man from the pressure of time and of making him time-free, a freedom that is actually tantamount to the new dimension itself. It is our task to see that the new dimension becomes a reality. The emergence of the fourth dimension in the consciousness will not drive out the existing magical, mythical, and mental dimensions, however. They remain valid and effective, but instead of being immoderate in their deficient form they will be there to the measure that they contribute to human harmony. It is for this reason that new consciousness is also known as "integral." In the fourth dimension we will be constantly aware of the whole, which is also the spiritual. One could also use Teilhard's term and refer to it as the Divine Milieu.

43

Hope in the Present Crisis: Transparency of the Divine in the New Man

Teilhard de Chardin perceived that evolution presses on toward the increasing perfection of man, which should be understood primarily in an anthropological and not in a moral sense. This process never reverses itself, and we are not even asked if we want what is coming. It just happens, and religions, too, must honor this. They must join with it and reorient themselves toward it. What is needed today is not new teachings, but new ways of expressing the same reality in accordance with the transformed consciousness. When a religion fails to allow this, it will not survive even though it may vegetate for a while longer with a few adherents. The president of the Club of Rome spoke about this at a meeting in Berlin in October 1979 when he said that the collected religions, concepts, principles, standpoints, assumptions, taboos, and value systems that determine our lives have grown old and unreliable. Mankind, he said, must finally realize how great the danger is so that it may come to its senses.

"Danger" here includes all the problems mentioned at the start of this book. But this danger is also the great hope of mankind, for it points to what is needed for liberation from the present threat. Whatever the future of the world may be, once this liberation is realized it will be a world where, to mention just one example, war will be rejected as a solution to political conflicts. We already know that modern wars increasingly take the form of conflicts where no side emerges as victor and all suffer serious damage. Present efforts to avoid war still founder due to a one-sided dualistic approach based on rational thinking. We will find a way out of such dilemmas when the world as a totality is present in the consciousness. Both sides will probably have to make great sacrifices. But this, too, can happen without bloodshed.

Of course, the world of the future will not be free of problems. The questions posed in the first pages of this book have not received satisfactory answers in any sense. But mankind will attain a unity in this new consciousness even while national borders still exist for the purposes of social order, until they too disappear. We can add here that the perfected man will have greater possibilities at his disposal. To realize this, we need only to compare the evolution from mythical to mental consciousness! Man of mythical consciousness, even in his wildest dreams, could have no idea of what his successors would eventually achieve in the area of technology alone. Thus it cannot be other than that the new man discovers new ways which we people of today cannot even imagine. Viewed in this way, man must take the step into the new consciousness or be condemned to oblivion. This most uncommon situation balances fear in the face of possible catastrophe against hope for a new age. That is in fact our present situation.

When anyone today speaks about the future, the emphasis is almost always on fear of what is coming. Perhaps we no longer have enough optimism to think seriously about the positive pole. Here Teilhard de Chardin is an exception. But for him the Omega point lies so far in the distance that people today cannot gain much encouragement from thinking about it. Perhaps modern man lacks the ability to "believe." Teilhard's vision does lie totally in the direction of Christian optimism, which itself depends on faith, not just on science, which also has its place in Teilhard's ideas.

Nevertheless, we should keep our eyes on what is to come once we prevail over the present crisis. This may be a better impulse toward action than fear of what is coming. For then the spiritual or the totality will be known permanently to us. With the new consciousness man will become a mystic, but one who awakens the mystical presence with the use of reason. This will be expressed in different ways depending on the particular religion, since the eye of enlightenment will be opened without individual effort. The new man will stand on a higher step than man of the mental structure, just as mental man stood on a higher step in comparison with mythical man. The importance of this becomes clear from the fact that we can say without exaggeration that this step will have a significance in human development second only to the evolution from animal to man. It will be greater than the crossover from mythical to mental consciousness. Whatever we may have to endure until the next step is completed will be worth it. Much which up to now has lain in the darkness of faith will become transparent. Contradictions will resolve themselves.

There have always been people who, through great suffering and extraordinary grace, have been able to attain to some extent that which will now become generally accessible. It will be a new humanity and a happier one. And yet we will retain everything bestowed upon us with our appearance in the world to the correct degree and in harmony with the whole. What Paul said to the Romans could become true in a new sense: ". . . be ye transformed by the renewing of your mind" (Rom. 12: 2).

> The profound Christian truth with regard to transparency, the diaphaneity of the world, becomes perceptible. The genuine irruption of the other side into this side, the presence of the beyond in the here and now, of death in life, of the transcendent in the immanent, of the divine in the human, becomes transparent. [Gebser, *The Ever-Present Origin*, p. 529]

44

The New Consciousness in Everyday Life

How will the new consciousness affect our daily lives? Its effects can become reality only when it is integrated by all of humanity. In other words, there will be a restructuring about which we can have no idea at present. But anyone who resists its influence will eventually be pushed aside.

Today there are still groups of people who have never left the stage of mythical consciousness. Science and technology will continue to develop, of course, even after integration of the new consciousness. But man, as the one who brought them into being, will be different from present-day man in terms of his consciousness. Freed of time, he will no longer suffer from the pressures felt by man of the mental structure.

Even after integral consciousness becomes a reality, man must struggle to free himself from imprisonment in an ego in order for the new consciousness to be consolidated, since freedom from the ego is characteristic of the new consciousness. When this work has been completed in ourselves our environment will correct itself, so to speak.

What can we do to find our way to the new consciousness? First, we must be aware that there *is* a new consciousness and believe in it. Unfortunately those who know about it and believe in it are still very few at present. One is reminded of Diogenes, who roamed the marketplace in broad daylight carrying a lighted lantern in his hand. Asked what he was doing, he replied, "I am looking for an honest man."

The world is already full of rumors, suppositions, and fears about a world catastrophe in the year 2000. But virtually no one knows what is actually happening. Those who do know are not believed, and so they keep silent.

Nevertheless, there are ways to encourage receptivity toward what is to come. One of these is meditation, which is much talked about these days. But ideally it should be a form of meditation that can be practiced in a nonrational and nonobjective way. The longing for this type of meditation is especially strong today in the West. This is a start since, when correctly practiced, nonobjective meditation moves in the direction of transcending the rational—although few people are presently aware of this connection. Most people meditate for other reasons: to be able to endure the stresses of modern life, or for some religious reason, such as reaching a deeper, nonrational level of prayer. One thing is certain, however; whether they realize it or not they all work for the new consciousness and thus for mankind as a whole. It is no coincidence that this great longing for nonobjective meditation has awakened at this time in the West, whose cultural sphere is founded on the rational. Western man apparently senses that rational thinking is no longer sufficient for being human in the deepest sense. The methods of nonobjective meditation can produce experiences that are characteristic of the new consciousness. Here it is naturally not possible to give a detailed explanation of each method. We will limit ourselves to a discussion of one method, Zen meditation, a method particularly well suited to this purpose since it excludes rationality from the beginning, which does not mean that it excludes or rejects rational thinking in all areas of life.

Enlightenment, the final goal of Zen, is an experience of the whole and overcomes the duality between man and world. The experience of oneness, of "becoming whole," is also a typical characteristic of integral consciousness. Even if only a few of those practicing this form of meditation should come to enlightenment, zazen (as Zen meditation is also called) can also help countless others to open themselves up to the new consciousness. At the same time, it encourages transparency, another characteristic of the new consciousness. This transparency first affects the individual in that the person's own unconsciousness becomes transparent. But transparency has effects on the external world as well. When the meditator is a Christian, he or she can gain a deeper understanding of the Scriptures through the practice of Zen, an understanding that goes beyond the rational without requiring detailed textual studies. The Christian liturgy can also become more accessible through meditation.

45

"Yes to Christ but No to the Church": The Search for the Dwelling Place of Divine Reality

However, because the Word (which is God) is inseparably bound with the historical Jesus, a new divine dimension is realized for humanity. Such a conclusion is justified by the fact that today, more than ever, we consider humanity to be a whole and not simply as the sum of many individuals— although the individual as such is always there, fully answerable for his actions. Speaking in a similar vein, Teilhard de Chardin says that the great mystery of Christianity is not the appearance but the transparency of God in the universe. We have already seen how transparency and nondualism are characteristic of the new consciousness.

We can understand religion as a universal phenomenon that was intimately involved with human history from the very start. But we can also approach it more individually and examine the different religions that have developed, finally applying our standards of evaluation to Christianity. When religion is regarded as a universal phenomenon, we are able to observe an evolution in the history of religion. This was the approach used in our discussion about the various structures of consciousness. From the perspective of these structures, Moses brought something new that was suitable for the prevailing circumstances of his time, particularly in consideration of the structures of consciousness then prevailing. The same holds for Buddha, Muhammad, and others. Mention can also be made here of the Vedic *rishis*, who were active at a much earlier time than the persons just mentioned. When this is also said concerning Christ, it is offensive to no one and thus such a claim is acceptable to non-Christians.

Jesus expressed this same thing in a way that his contemporaries could understand. For example, there are such well-known statements as "I and the Father are one" (John 10:30) and the words with which he bade farewell to his disciples before his passion and death: "He that hath seen me hath seen the Father" (John 14:9). Such declarations used the metaphor of a father-son relationship and were immediately understood by his listeners, not only by the apostles but also by his enemies, who wanted to stone him for blaspheming God when he said, "I and the Father are one."

In another pronouncement, Christ stated who he is without using a father-son simile: "I am the light of the world. He that followeth me shall not walk in darkness, but shall have the light of life" (John 8:12). Such words have probably never been spoken by anyone else before or since. If we understand these scriptural passages, we also understand why Jesus of Nazareth could speak in this way without presumption. Jean Gebser connects this claim with the mental structure of consciousness:

> With that declaration the first wholly self-assured resplendence of mankind breaks forth, a resplendence venturing to state for the first time that it will assume the burden of the world's darkness and suffering. [Gebser, *The Ever-Present Origin,* p. 90]

From the perspective of the unfolding of consciousness, this obviously signals an intensification. At the same time, it heralds a new view of suffering, which differs from the Four Noble Truths preached some six hundred years earlier by the Buddha: "Life is suffering. Suffering has causes (desire). The causes of suffering can be extinguished. There is a path by which we can extinguish suffering." Christianity took the way indicated by Christ, a man who had taken the suffering of the world upon himself and attempted to overcome it with love of the world. When Christ said, "I am the light of the world," there was a special emphasis on the words "am" and "world." He is not the one who enlightens but rather the light itself. "World" means what is outside, in other words, humanity.

Once the new consciousness has been truly integrated, much will be fulfilled in a Christian sense, too. It has been said, for example, that there will be an end to all war, and this time a true ending. Already in the Old Testament there are prophecies concerning eternal peace. Isaiah prophesied among other things that "they shall beat their swords into plowshares and their spears into pruninghooks: nation shall not lift up sword against nation, neither shall they learn war any more" (Isaiah 2:4).

These predictions concerned the coming messianic kingdom. But the fulfillment of such prophecies is not to be sought in terms of a particular day or year. We can see the beginning of a transformation of the world, fullfilling the messianic prophecies, in all that will be realized in the integral consciousness. Even the eventual immortality of the body is basically not opposed to Christian teaching. The body has a human essence and thus participates, according to the Christian understanding, in the glorification of the spirit even when this does not happen within a certain calculable period of time, as Aurobindo understood it, but rather comes to fulfillment "at the end of time."

But let us return to the present, since this hour of the world is of special significance for the Christian. The more the effects of the new consciousness are felt, the more Christianity will fall into a state of crisis, particularly the churches. The following is offered as a partial explanation for this. Christianity traces its beginnings back to the cultural and religious milieu of Palestine some two thousand years ago. Christ and his disciples came from that land and almost without exception were indigenous to that culture. The apostles did not journey to Athens and Rome to first integrate the cultures there and then finally preach Christianity to the world in accordance with Christ's directions. Nevertheless, the theology that developed from the teachings of Christ had an extremely close relationship with Greco-Roman culture and later with medieval scholasticism. Recently, all of these cultural relationships have come into question, along with much else. The Second Vatican Council, the immortal contribution of Pope John XXIII, was convened to take these developments into account. Since then, much has been done and much has occurred to do justice to continuing changes.

To this we can add the fact that today even religious orders, which have done so much over the centuries to spread and deepen Christianity, have come into question. The distinction between clerical and "the world," between sacred and profane, is no longer relevant. The same holds for the division between clergy and faithful. Since the Second Vatican Council it has been continually emphasized that all Christians are basically the same, even when, for practical reasons, the areas of responsibility within the Church are still somewhat divided. Some may ask regarding this whether the traditional form of religious orders is in keeping with the times. Many critics go so far as to reject all forms of community, not only religious orders but churches as well. Such a wholesale rejection is neither in keeping with the nature of the human being nor with religion itself, since neither is merely an individual matter but primarily a communal one. It is more a question of finding new forms of community life that are in keeping with the times.

Because of its extremely systematized forms based on the rational structures of Western thinking, Christianity will probably be more seriously affected by the integration of the new consciousness than most other religions. Integration of the new consciousness is not simply a matter of replacing an old system with a new one. On the contrary, systems and other categorical or perspectival ways of thinking would only serve to block the integration process. On the other hand—and this is the bright side of this dilemma—one result of the new consciousness is that solutions will occur to us by themselves. This will also be true for the unification of Christians, something that has been sought so long. In like manner, relationships between the religions of the world will become closer and easier as the tensions that still exist today gradually resolve themselves.

What Christianity will look like after the total integration of the new consciousness among humanity is something no one can foretell at present. But we should ask ourselves now what can be done so that the appropriate new forms can be found. Something we can say at the outset is that we must return to the sources, to Christ and the apostles who lived with him. Yet it is believed that even the evangelists represent a further development, so that the source waters were muddied even then. Even in those earlier times there were other accounts of Christ and his teachings. Here we will only mention briefly the Gospel according to Thomas, a document whose discovery a few decades ago aroused great interest. Then, however, it was declared to be inauthentic. Even if it was not written by the apostle Thomas, it does originate from the early days of Christianity and thus has an individual stamp. It is a short text, and what survives is probably just a fragment of the entire Gospel. The statements of Christ found within it often remind one of Zen koans.

Be that as it may, one thing must always be remembered. Beginning with the apostles and continuing with the teachings of the Church and those of the individual denominations, there has never been any other task than for us to come into contact with the sources, that is, with Christ himself and his teachings and his experience as God-man. This conviction has in fact never been so clear and convincing as today. "Christ, yes—Church, no" has already become a catchword of our times, although whether it is justified or not remains undetermined. But precisely because everything that came into being in the meantime has come into question, we now find it so extraordinarily difficult to pinpoint the sources. What assurance is there that what we find in our search for the sources is truly the teaching and experience of Christ? If there is any assurance, it can only lie in the individual religious experience encountered in deep prayer and contemplation. It is only here that the answer has a chance of coming directly from Christ. And it is for this reason that the search for sources and new forms must always be closely bound with religious experience.

46

The Cloud of Unknowing: Coming to Our Spiritual Home in Everyday Life

Consciously or unconsciously, Western man seeks the ultimate and the exclusively valid, which can only be God. The earliest catechetical instruction should include a chapter on the experience of God and on meditation. So long as this is lacking, we cannot do justice to the particular individuality of the new man. In short, anyone who wants to be Christian in the fullest sense of the word, and who uses meditation as a means to this end, must sooner or later arrive at a form of meditation that is practiced in the core of the soul rather than merely on the surface of the spirit. Whether we can reach this goal without meditation is, at the very least, doubtful, given the present religious situation. At any rate, the transformation of the person required for this process must penetrate to the very core of the soul.

This brings us to the following questions: How do we come to the spiritual state where this meditation can begin? What blocks us from the path to this form of meditation? As early as six hundred years ago, the author of a short mystical tract entitled *The Cloud of Unknowing* tried to answer these questions. The name of the author, apparently an English Carthusian monk, remains unknown. Nevertheless, it is almost certain that he is also the author of other writings that have come down to us, among them *The Book of Privy Counsel*. This work is in the form of a dialogue that answers questions that might arise while practicing the method described in *The*

Cloud, and therefore it is of great value for a more complete understanding of *The Cloud.* Although *The Cloud of Unknowing* was written in the fourteenth century, the essence of what is prescribed therein remains valid today. And although it introduces a wholly Christian meditation method, it bears striking similarities with many Eastern methods. Here we shall introduce and briefly discuss its main points.

Without doubt, the book attempts a methodical instruction for mystical prayer. In accordance with this, its author warns in his foreword that whoever reads this document or has it read to him must be someone who "over and above the good works of the active life, has resolved to follow Christ (as far as is humanly possible with God's grace) into the inmost depths of contemplation" (trans. William Johnston, Garden City, New York, 1973, p. 43). On the other hand, the author says that anyone who has practiced the usual methods of contemplation for a period of time will be able to make this new method his own if he fulfills the necessary conditions.

The "cloud of unknowing" refers to the sphere existing between God and man, which we must penetrate in order to come to God in the sense of an experience of Him. Concretely speaking, this means that we must forget all the knowledge that we possess, even knowledge of one's self. Thus we should not dwell upon even those tenets of faith that formerly we may have meditated on to our great consolation and help.

> It is equally useless to think you can nourish your contemplation work by considering God's attributes, his kindness or his dignity; or by thinking about our Lady, the angels, or the saints.   [trans. Johnston, p. 54]

On the contrary:

> Reject the thought and experience of all created things but most especially learn to forget yourself, for all your knowledge and experience depends upon the knowledge and feeling of yourself. All else is easily

forgotten in comparison with one's own self. See if your experience does not prove me right. Long after you have successfully forgotten every creature and its works, you will find that a naked knowing and feeling of your own being still remains between you and your God. And believe me, you will not be perfect in love until this, too, is destroyed.   [pp. 102–103]

What is to be rejected is "all thought." This includes not only everything bad or opposed to our goal, such as evil tendencies and sin, but also quite simply everything created, even if it is good. One might conclude that such a method deprives, in a sense, everything created of its value, which would not be in keeping with the Christian view of creation. However, in *The Cloud of Unknowing* we are concerned not with this problem but rather—as we say today—with an emptying of the consciousness or the mind. Thus, rejecting all thought must include all thoughts of a religious nature to the extent that they are conceptual knowledge or take the form of images in the imagination such as are activated in objective meditation. Even theoretical knowledge about God must be forgotten. Needless to say, since the author of *The Cloud* lived in times different from our own, he does not speak in terms of emptying the consciousness. Nevertheless, this is actually what is involved. The first precondition for application of this method, an honest striving for purity of heart, remains valid for all times. It would be presumptuous to strive for deeper and more perfect prayer without striving at the same time to become free from sin and dissolute practices. For striving of this sort aims at approaching God while sin leads us away from God. They are two motions that are opposed to each other and would therefore cancel each other out. As an old Master once put it, you cannot eat at the same table with God and the devil.

As far as emptying the consciousness is concerned, these instructions agree in many respects with Eastern methods.

This holds especially for Zen, in which all meditation objects are rejected from the very beginning without any preliminary form of objective meditation. The foundation in both methods is the same, since both involve a striving toward a higher form of knowledge. In the Christian context, this means that the knowledge we have possessed up to now is conceptual and limited, whereas God is beyond concepts and unlimited. No human concept can comprehend God. As long as God is being grasped in concepts, it is an idol, and not God, that we are describing. Thus, as long as we attempt to approach God with concepts taken from the limited world of creation, he will elude us. It is like trying to grasp the air. More concretely, we may not allow ourselves any type of thinking during meditation, whether it be self-induced thoughts or thoughts that we hold on to when they enter our consciousness by chance. We should not permit the entrance of any thought, good or bad. Such "not-thinking" is extremely difficult for Westerners, because our entire culture is based so preponderantly on thinking. Nevertheless, as long as we consciously and willfully think, the other powers that are awakened in nonobjective meditation cannot come into action.

Clearly the author of *The Cloud* was very aware of the difficulties involved in this practice, even when we drop all the theoretical misgivings we might have and apply ourselves to it diligently. For this reason, he recommends that we choose a word and use it to drive away all the thoughts that press in upon our consciousness. Ideally the word should be a short one such as "God" or "Praise." It doesn't even need to be religious in content as long as it is short. It is a shield or spear with which we drive away every thought. What we are advised to do here is not identical, however, with what happens when meditating on a scriptural passage or using a mantra in the manner advised in many Indian forms of meditation. Nor is it the same as the koan used to achieve a similar purpose in Zen.

The author of *The Cloud* says it is so difficult to root out all knowledge and feelings about any particular creation, particularly one's own self, that it surpasses human ability; it is possible only with the help of God. If this was true for people in the Middle Ages, a time when people were far more disposed to meditation than now, how much more difficult it must be for us in the twentieth century. Thus we must look for a new means that will come to our aid and allow us to prevail over the particular difficulties of our confused times. In the process, we should consider first the means at our disposal right now, such as correct sitting posture and proper breathing. It is completely consistent with Christian practice to place the body in the service of the religious element; this has always been the case during the liturgy. The body is just as much a part of being a person as the spirit and thus should be healed with the spirit. In fact, a transformation has recently occurred in Christian spirituality regarding our understanding of the relationship between the body and the spirit. Although people of earlier times often considered the body to be a hindrance to activating the spirit in a religious sense, people of today tend more toward the view of body and spirit as a unified whole. A new understanding is gradually prevailing which makes no sharp separation between the two.

Hugo M. Enomiya-Lassalle
A Biographical Sketch

Hugo Lassalle was born on 11 November 1898 in Externbrock bei Nieheim, Westphalia. He comes from an old Huguenot family; hence his French name. Lassalle attended school in Hildesheim and the Petrinum Gymnasium in Brilon from 1911 to 1916. Drafted for military service in November 1916, he fought on the Western front, was wounded in October 1917, and was discharged in 1919.

Lassalle entered the North German provinciate of the Jesuit order on 25 April 1919 and from 1919 to 1921 was a resident of the Jesuit novitiate house in s'Heerenberg in the Netherlands. From 1921 to 1924 he studied philosophy at the Ignatian College in Valkenburg, the Netherlands, and in Stonyhurst, England. Theological studies took place between 1924 and 1928 in Valkenburg and at Heythrop College near Oxford. He was ordained on 28 August 1927 and spent his tertiate in Amiens, France, from 1928 to 1929.

Arriving in Japan in 1929, Father Lassalle was first active in Tokyo, where he taught German at Sophia University, a Jesuit institution. During this period he joined his students in dedicating his spare hours to social work in the slums of Tokyo, where in 1931 he founded the welfare project known as Jochi Settlement. From 1935 to 1949, Father Lassalle was Superior of the Jesuit Mission in Japan, and in this capacity he attended the General Assembly of his order held in Rome in 1938. His duties at this time included trips to Germany, England, Canada, and the United States on behalf of the Japanese mission.

Father Lassalle left Tokyo in 1938 for Nagatsuka, near

Hiroshima, where he was in charge of the Jesuit novitiate. In 1940 he moved to Hiroshima and acted as Vicarium Delegatus of the Apostolic Curacy there from 1940 to 1959. During this time and afterward until 1962, Father Lassalle also served as a parish priest, did missionary work, and taught German at the higher normal school and the cadet academy. He was wounded in the atomic bomb attack on 6 August and has since suffered the effects of radiation.

A second trip to the General Congress of his order was followed by visits to Germany, France, Switzerland, Spain, South America, and the United States during 1946–47. In talks delivered during those visits, Father Lassalle pleaded for understanding toward Japan and promoted the building of a "Church of World Peace" in Hiroshima, a project for which he received assistance both from abroad and in Japan, from Christians and non-Christians alike. Funds for the structure were also collected door-to-door in the city of Hiroshima itself. All major Japanese companies and banks participated in the drive, and diplomats stationed in Japan also assisted. The cornerstone was laid on 6 August 1950 and the church was dedicated on 6 August 1954. Without Father Lassalle's tireless efforts, the city that arose newborn from the ashes of death might never have become a "mecca of world peace."

From 1950 to 1978 (when he turned eighty) Father Lassalle continued to be active as professor of religion at the St. Elizabeth College of Music in Hiroshima. Because of his ties to the country where he had lived and worked the longest, Father Lassalle took on Japanese citizenship in 1948 and assumed the Japanese name Makibi Enomiya. In recognition of his outstanding contributions to the cause of peace and reconciliation, he was designated an honorary citizen of Hiroshima by that city on 1 April 1968.

In 1962, Father Lassalle turned over his duties of curate at the Church of World Peace in Hiroshima to a diocesan priest and that same year accompanied the bishop of Hiroshima as his personal secretary to attend the Second Vatican Council in Rome.

Of particular importance in Father Lassalle's life was his encounter with Zen meditation. In 1943 he participated for the first time in a seven-day sesshin held at Eimyoji, a temple in Tsuwano, Shimane prefecture. Already during the war he dedicated himself to Zen training and practiced under Harada Daiun Sogaku Roshi, one of the most well-known Zen masters of his day.

Enomiya-Lassalle discovered Zen for Christianity. No missionary in Japan has experienced the practice of Zen so intensively as he. Although at first he practiced Zen for his own spiritual development, he later happened on the idea of teaching these practices to others. He had been looking for a key to the Japanese spirit and found it in Zen. The more he devoted himself to Zen, initially to gain access to the heart of Japan, the more he experienced how Zen was an outstanding aid to his own religious life as a Catholic priest. As he put it, in Zen the soul advances toward God up to the limits of its possibilities. Personal ambition is foreign to this simple, unassuming, and self-possessed man.

In 1967, after attending the East-West Encounter at Elmau Castle in West Germany, Enomiya-Lassalle gave talks on Zen at various locations in West Germany. In 1968—having relocated to Tokyo and the newly-founded Institute of Oriental Religions at Sophia University—he returned once more to Germany and directed his first Zen sesshins in the secluded settings of the Benedictine monasteries at Niederaltaich, Weingarten, and Maria Laach. Since then, Enomiya-Lassalle has held Zen sesshins annually in Europe, where he now spends three-quarters of the year. Although there is no publicity, the Zen courses are always fully booked; applications made a year in advance are by no means rare.

Enomiya-Lassalle's creative energy and tireless dedication are without precedent. In Japan, too, he is active as a Zen teacher. In 1960, the bishop of Hiroshima dedicated Shinmeikutsu ("Cave of Divine Darkness"), a small Zen meditation house near Hiroshima constructed by Father Lassalle. In 1969 the archibishop of Tokyo dedicated Akikawa-Shinmeikutsu, a Zen hall created by Enomiya-Lassalle in a secluded nature preserve on the outskirts of Tokyo. Surrounded on three sides by a rushing stream known as Akikawa (literally "Autumn River"), the "Cave of Divine Darkness" is the first Christian Zen meditation center in Japan. It is so named because the light of enlightenment breaks forth from the mysterious darkness like a bolt of lightning in a pitch-black night.

Since the late sixties, Enomiya-Lassalle has been conducting regular sesshins in Europe and Japan while also finding time for trips to the cultural centers of Buddhism and other Eastern religions in Korea, India, Thailand, and the United States. Between 1974 and 1977 he conducted sesshins in Vietnam, the Philippines, Hong Kong, Taiwan, and Pakistan.

On 17 December 1977, Enomiya-Lassalle formally opened a new Zen meditation hall in a Franciscan monastery in Dietfurt (near Munich), after its dedication by the bishop of Eichstatt. Lasalle's numerous publications attest to his experience in Zen while explaining the theory and practice of Zen from a Christian standpoint. These works are now available in several languages.

Although Lassalle's first book, *Zen-Weg zur Erleuchtung* (1960), was first objected to by the Church because of "heretical tendencies," it was later removed from the Index during the Second Vatican Council, an event that has helped to open a window on the East. Father Pedro Arrupe, director general of the Jesuit order for many years, writes as follows about his fellow Jesuit: "Because I know Father Lassalle very well both from without and from within, I feel I can say that he is no 'guru,' no 'leader,' no 'spiritual father,' no 'romantic,' no 'worldly Jesuit.' No, he is all that and much more. He is an apostle who wished to 'become all things to all men' (2 Cor. 9:22) and who has succeeded in that task."

Zen masters in Japan consider Jesuit and Zen master Hugo Makibi Enomiya-Lassalle as their equal.

A Note on Zen Sesshin

Zen sesshin are days devoted to spiritual concentration and the intensive practice of zazen under an authentic Zen master. During sesshin under the direction of Father Lassalle, usually from five to nine days in length, absolute silence reigns, even during mealtimes. Every moment is devoted solely to spiritual practice.

Participants in a Zen sesshin are not permitted to read or listen to radio or watch television. Such distractions would have the effect of diverting the practitioner from the goal. Each day during sesshin, the master gives a one-hour talk (*teisho*), and participants are also free to come regularly to the master for a private interview, known as *dokusan*. This interview gives the student an opportunity to report to the teacher on experiences and difficulties during Zen practice and to ask questions about how to practice more effectively. Practiced diligently, the Zen way can eventually lead to enlightenment.

A typical day at a Zen sesshin with Father Lassalle would be as follows:

6:00 A.M.	Rise
6:30	Tea
6:45	Zazen (three 30-minute periods)
8:30	Breakfast
9:00	Cleanup
10:00	Coffee or tea
10:20	Teisho
11:20	Zazen (three 30-minute periods)
1:00 P.M.	Dinner and midday break
3:00	Zazen (four 30-minute periods)
5:20	Supper
6:30	Celebration of the Eucharist
7:25	Zazen (three 30-minute periods)
9:00	Retire